T0114210

I WAS BORN THIS WAY

A GAY PREACHER'S JOURNEY THROUGH GOSPEL MUSIC, DISCO STARDOM, AND A MINISTRY IN CHRIST

ARCHBISHOP CARL BEAN
with DAVID RITZ

SIMON & SCHUSTER
New York   London   Toronto   Sydney

Simon & Schuster
1230 Avenue of the Americas
New York, NY 10020

First Simon & Schuster hardcover edition June 2010

SIMON & SCHUSTER and colophon are registered trademarks
of Simon & Schuster, Inc.

For information about special discounts for bulk purchases,
please contact Simon & Schuster Special Sales at 1-866-506-1949
or business@simonandschuster.com.

The Simon & Schuster Speakers Bureau can bring authors
to your live event. For more information or to book an event
contact the Simon & Schuster Speakers Bureau at 1-866-248-3049
or visit our website at www.simonspeakers.com.

Designed by Esther Paradelo

Unless otherwise noted, all insert photographs courtesy of Rev. Carl Bean.

Manufactured in the United States of America

10   9   8   7   6   5   4   3   2   1

Library of Congress Cataloging-in-Publication Data
Bean, Carl, vocalist.
  I was born this way : a gay preacher's journey through gospel music,
  disco stardom, and a ministry in Christ / Carl Bean with David Ritz.—1st
  Simon & Schuster hardcover ed.
    p.   cm.
  1. Bean, Carl, vocalist. 2. African American clergy—Biography.
  3. Singers—United States—Biography. 4. African American gays—Biography.
  I. Ritz, David. II. Title.
  BR563.N4B43 2010
  277.3'082092—dc22
  [B]
                        2009033504

ISBN 978-1-4165-9283-9

Dedicated to the village, that sacred phenomenon
of black life in America that nurtured me,
sustained me, and continues to inform my heart.

And to the Creator, thank you for placing me in this body,
this skin, this orientation, this life that you have guided
every step of the way.

PROLOGUE

I begin in the streets of my childhood in Baltimore. I remember the joy and love. We were all related by blood, common experience, or mutual care. I was a little feminine creature, a soft boy with a big heart and an even bigger need to love and be loved. The village gave me that love. It was filled with characters—card-players and garbagemen, hairdressers and seamstresses, car mechanics and factory workers, domestics, teachers, and preachers, people from the South who came to Baltimore and did their best to adjust to the brick-hard reality of urban life.

My neighbor Mrs. Jordan, sensing I wanted to help, showed me how to scrub her stoop. While we scrubbed, she talked about Lionel Hampton and the man called Charlie "Yardbird" Parker. Other neighbors, like Mr. and Mrs. Wise, had Duke Ellington records on 78 vinyl discs that they played for me. I loved going over to Aunt Nellie's. She wasn't a blood relative but treated me like one. At her house, I learned to read music, read magazines like *National Geographic*, and cut fried chicken to the bone. Aunt Nellie was an elementary school teacher who later became a principal. She and her husband, Uncle Andrew, had no children. An oil painting of their dog Chubby hung over their fireplace. There was Ms. Florence, whose skin was whitening and turning her into an albino and who always had time for me. Mr. Johnson, with his secret stack of nude-ladies playing cards; the drum majors in their fabulous costumes; Jewish merchants like Morris Ginsberg, whose wife taught me words in a strange language called Yiddish.

And there I was—singing doo-wop with the boys, jumping double Dutch with the girls, shooting marbles, moving from house to house where I was always welcomed, wanted, and appreciated. They saw my girlish ways and never once chided me. I never felt the need to hide in a closet. I thrived among my people. They gave me the emotional stamina to be me—the authentic me.

Looking back, I see that the village was founded on the love of God.

God was there before I knew what to call that spirit.

God was there to convey the unspoken words that I heard not in my ears but in my heart: *It's all right. You're all right. Yes, Carl, you're safe.*

Among the poorest of the poor, among the frightened and the lonely, among the scorned and rejected, among families that were broken and on the brink of destruction, God was there.

God was there in my eyes as I looked at the world around me.

Baltimore, Maryland, 1947, a city of row houses. A city marked by strict racial and social divisions. And a city within a city where a people, cut off from all wealth and privilege, struggled to survive.

The creator was there as I, a chubby child, sat on those worn marble steps and felt sounds coming across my vocal cords. God was there in my voice as I started to sing the first few notes.

I hadn't been to church all that often, but often enough to fall in love with God's music. As I stood up and started marching, singing all the way, I pretended to be a member of the choir walking down the main aisle while women in wide-brimmed hats waved handkerchiefs and cried out, "Sing, boy! Go on and sing!" In reality I was walking down the alley between the two houses that would define my childhood.

Once in that same alley I found an old beat-up umbrella. I tore the black nylon material from its frame and threw it over my shoulders. This was my robe. I was singing God's praises before I knew what those words meant.

God was in my mouth, in my song, in my make-believe.

I can't tell you why I felt this connection to God.

I can't tell you why I picked up that tiny ant crawling on the pavement and placed it in the palm of my hand. Why in that creature did I feel a connection to all things? Why did that connection give me a joy that had no name—a joy that kept me calm when I had every reason to be crazy?

Why did I see God in the ant?

Why did I see God in the little green buds on the branches of a scraggly old tree?

Why did I see God in the puffy gray clouds racing across the sky?

Why did I feel God in the first drops of gentle rain falling on my face?

God was with my family when we assembled in the living room to watch the gathering storm.

He was there when the lightning cracked and the thunder rolled.

The elders turned off the radio—even to interrupt their favorite program—and said, "God is speaking through the storm." The elders believed that God was alive in the power of the storm. The elders prayed silently while we children sat in reverence until the storm passed.

THE TWO HOUSES

I was born in Baltimore, Maryland, on May 26, 1944.

Mom was fifteen, Dad was sixteen, and they never married.

Twenty-nine years earlier, Billie Holiday was born in the same neighborhood of the same city and raised by a single mother. She began her autobiography by saying, "Mom and Dad were just a couple of kids when they got married. He was eighteen, she was sixteen, and I was three." I have always loved the immortal jazz singer as someone who came from these same streets, my precious soul sister, a wounded healer who could turn pain into beauty and, in doing so, inspire us to do the same.

I was raised by many mothers who took me in and loved me completely. These warm and wonderful women made me strong.

My upbringing was not conventional, but it was typical of how black families, who moved up to great urban centers from the rural South, coped with domestic circumstances. The responsibility of caring for children was often shared among family and nonfamily members alike.

My biological father, Calvin, was not ready for fatherhood. He had little or no interest in raising a kid.

My biological mother, Arlene, did her best. She and her mom, her two sisters, and three brothers all lived in a small row house on Dallas Street in East Baltimore. Mom's dad had separated from the family and lived a few blocks away on Fayette Street. Dallas Street was the first house I lived in.

The kids in our neighborhood flowed from house to house and were watched over by virtually everyone. My teenage mother was loving, but she had a full-time job and a circle of young friends. Her sisters, brothers, and mother, though, were always looking after me. We were also protected and even disciplined by people who acted—out of love and concern—on behalf of our blood relatives.

Just as the row houses were all connected, so were our families. I loved the connections. This is how we survived.

More than any institution, the church ensured our survival. As we came up from slavery and went through Reconstruction, we suffered the indignities and larcenies of sharecropping. Moving into the big cities, we had nowhere to look for a sense of self-worth, and the church, for all its shortcomings and hypocrisies, instilled within us a sense of pride. In God's eyes, we were as important and loved as everyone else. We were taught in Matthew 25:45 that "Whatever you did not do for the least of these, you did not do for me."

My church experience began when, at age three, I attended United Baptist with my mom and our neighbor Miss Nazarene. Mom would wear a chignon woven into her hair. One time, as the music started pumping and the reverend started preaching, Mom got so happy and jumped so high that the chignon came loose and started rolling down the center aisle. I chased after it, running as fast as I could while everyone shouted and laughed.

Miss Nazarene sang with the choir. I could see her up in the choir loft, could identify her big beautiful alto, and was able to sing along in tune. Someone heard me, told the lady choir director, and suddenly I was rehearsing with the junior choir. When the choir director said, "Little Carl is going to sing for us," I was too bashful to utter a sound. She asked the entire choir to go outside. Imagine—she took such an interest in me that she disrupted her rehearsal.

"Just sing, honey," she said. "Sing for me."

I sang my heart out, but when the other kids came back, my shyness returned. I stayed silent. Eventually, though, the director's gentle encouragement gave me the courage to sing with the choir. And once I started, I never stopped.

Back home, I sang those church songs as I watched the ladies on our block scrub the old marble steps in front of every row house. There was tremendous pride in our neighborhood, even a summertime competition among streets called Clean Blocks. Whose street could be cleaner and prettier? If we found discarded tires, we'd place them at the edge of the curb and plant flower seeds in them. Every morning I'd run down and water the soil, waiting and watching for any sign of growth. The first little bloom was cause for celebration.

Meanwhile, I spent time in two main places, my birth mother's house and the home of Harry and Jeter Smith next door. The Smiths didn't have children together. I considered them my godparents and called them Uncle Harry and Aunt Dee. Harry had a daughter named Martha, who was three years older than me and lived across the street with her mama, Aunt Edie. Martha and I were—and still are—as close as any sister and brother could possibly be. Aunt Dee's mama also took to me. Her name was Stagey Gaines, but I called her Nana.

Nana was the one who looked after me during the day and rocked me to sleep at night. Nana made me feel safe. She had come up from Virginia and was solid as the earth and bright as the sky. Nana was a proud southern lady who went to church every Sunday at Israel Baptist on Orleans Street wearing her pink and black suit and pink-feathered hat.

On Orleans Street she'd point her finger and say, "Now if

9

you go in that direction, Sammy"—Sammy was my nickname— "you'll find all the homes of those white folk where my daughter cooks and cleans. Go in the other direction and you'll be downtown in no time."

Holding my hand, she walked into that church as if she owned it. We always sat on the very first pew. I was convinced that Nana had a direct line to God. She was, after all, a deaconess in his church. She was also a member in good standing of the Order of the Eastern Star. On special occasions, she'd wear her uniform and fez. When the Eastern Star took over church, the entire neighborhood would be abuzz. The pageantry was brilliant.

After church, we went home and Nana cooked up a storm. Then came the weekly chores: on Monday she washed; Tuesday and Wednesday, she would pull out her smoothing iron and press down the clothes. Saturday we cleaned from the attic to the front steps. Then before bedtime she put me in a number ten tub, soaped me up, scrubbed me down, and dried me off. At bedtime, I loved her Bible stories about David and Goliath or Jesus calling the children to his side.

If I got into trouble by playing on the streets too long or falling in the mud and dirtying my shirt, I ran to Nana. Nana felt more like my mama than my mama.

When summer came, Nana canned preserves—peaches, pears, and grape jelly in big Mason jars. I loved to sit by Nana's side and watch as the iceman arrived carrying a big block of ice. Nana fixed me a cold drink and made me a sandwich. When the sun went down, I sat at the kitchen table and stared at the radio, as if pictures were emerging from that small miraculous box. *Stella Dallas, The Fat Man, The Jack Benny Show,* and *I Remember Mama.* Sometimes Nana turned the dial to find the Wings Over Jordan Choir singing the spirituals she loved so much. In the forties, Wings Over Jordan was the most popular church group in black America.

As the sun was setting, Nana pointed out the window to her daughter Aunt Dee, who was walking up the street toward the house, and said, "Look who's coming, Sammy."

I ran outside into Aunt Dee's waiting arms. From the private homes where she worked, Aunt Dee always had a cookie or piece of cake for me. Unlike her mother, though, Aunt Dee said few words. She stuttered severely, and her impediment turned her shy.

In one house or the other, I was a happy child, but it was surely Nana who made me happiest. Her very physical presence—she was a great big strong woman—gave me the feeling of safety. In the color of her skin and the shape of her facial features, you could see the Native American blood that she spoke about. Every August, Nana, Uncle Harry, Aunt Dee, Martha, and I drove down to Virginia for Nana's Harvest Homecoming Rally, where she was treated like a queen. Many of her relatives had the same Native American/African American characteristics—the thick wavy hair, the rounded nose, the ruby-tinted skin tone. I wasn't a blood relative, but at those church picnics I was treated like one.

Back in Baltimore, Nana, along with her daughter Jeter, bought me little church suits and dressed me like a little prince. Nana often took me to the funeral parlor where she fixed the hair of ladies who had passed. Mr. Elroy, a gentleman with light skin and wavy hair, owned the establishment. I carefully watched as Nana put wigs on the deceased ladies' heads or styled their hair with a curling iron. I also attended the funerals themselves, which fascinated me.

The ritual always included the local gospel singer, a lady of strong voice and confident manner. As she sang, Nana hummed along while I, by Nana's side, joined in. I saw the deep respect given to the grieving family, especially the grieving widow, whose face was covered by a long thick veil. The women dressed in black dresses, black shoes, black hats. The men wore dark suits with black hearts sewn on the sleeves. For the final viewing, Nana and the singer stood on either side of the widow, carefully lifted her veil, and accompanied her to the casket. Meanwhile, the singer shouted out "Oh, When I Come to the End of My Journey," repeating the lyrics again and again until everyone had a chance to view the body. At that age, I didn't understand the deep grief, but I felt the beauty of the pageantry. I was moved by Nana's dignity and strength. Death didn't frighten her.

Death frightened me. A year later, an ambulance took Nana to nearby Johns Hopkins Hospital. When Uncle Harry and Aunt Dee brought me to visit her, the big marble statue of Jesus in the lobby nearly scared me to death. Nana looked awful, groaning every time she moved. I knew something was terribly wrong, but no one would say what. When they brought Nana home, her chest was covered with bandages. As they carried her inside, she reached out to me. "Sammy," she said. I took her hand, but then they carried her into the room and the door closed. I banged, but they wouldn't let me in. When I heard Nana crying, I started crying as well.

"It's all right, baby," I heard her say through the door.

For days, I'd sit in front of the closed door, listening to her moans. When Aunt Dee or a neighbor walked out of the room, I tried to run in, but they stopped me.

"She needs quiet," they said. "She needs peace."

And then one day, after weeks of being separated from Nana, I watched them carry her out of her room. This time there was a white sheet covering her entire body. I couldn't see her face.

"Where are you taking her?" I asked Uncle Harry.

"To Mr. Elroy's," he said.

I was confused and afraid.

What did this mean?

Everyone in both houses—my mother's and Uncle Harry's—went to the funeral parlor. They surrounded me as we walked into the room with the coffin, where Nana lay in one of her favorite church dresses, a smile on her face.

"They laid her out beautifully," I heard someone say.

She did look beautiful, but she wasn't moving, and at that moment, I understood that she would never move again.

"Breast cancer," I overheard one of Nana's relatives say. "Breast cancer took her."

The next day, I was in the back of Uncle Harry's black Buick as we drove down to Richmond County, Virginia, for the funeral held at Mulberry Baptist Church. After the service, I went to the church graveyard and watched them lay Nana to rest.

On the ride home, I cried my little eyes out. I was inconsolable. I couldn't deal with the idea that I'd never see Nana again—never be in the kitchen with her while she lovingly prepared our evening meal; never hear her tell me Bible stories at night.

Sensing my deep grief, Aunt Dee whispered in my ear, "You're with us now, Sammy."

"We're getting a new house," Uncle Harry added.

"We have a bedroom just for you," said Aunt Dee. "We're going to take care of you, Sammy. We're always going to take care of you."

I was having a second and very different emotional experience at the time of Nana's death. I had my first crush. I wasn't even five when I fell in love with a boy with soft waves in his hair, eyes like brown embers, coal black skin, and a smile that warmed my heart. He lived nearby, and his name was also Karl*. He fascinated me. I loved looking at him from across the street. I loved being with him. I was fixated on his laugh and the way he

* Indicates fictitious name

spoke my name. "Sammy," he'd say, "let's play." That's all I needed to hear. My relatives couldn't help but see my fondness for Karl, but they never criticized me. Maybe they thought I'd grow out of it. Instead, I grew even more infatuated.

Increasingly, the adults most responsible for me were Uncle Harry and Aunt Dee. When they moved into their new row house on Jefferson Street, they took me with them. It was there that I had a bedroom of my own. There wasn't any farewell scene with Arlene, my natural mother. She must have seen that I'd have a better life with Uncle Harry and Aunt Dee. To allow them to raise her son was an act of generosity and love. It all happened naturally.

A few weeks after moving in, I was playing outside with some friends when Uncle Harry came to the front door and shouted my name.

"Your dad's calling you," said one of my little buddies.

That's when Uncle Harry became Dad and Aunt Dee became Mom. Mom was unable to have kids of her own. She adored children and, along with her mother, Nana, had been drawn to me since the day I was born. She was also related to my natural dad's family: Calvin's mother was married to Aunt Dee's brother. So my paternal grandmother and newly adopted mom were sisters-in-law and as close as blood sisters. In fact, it was my grandmother who had helped care for Nana.

Although Baltimore was—and remains—a city with a large impoverished black community, by virtue of this adoption I was blessed to have a magnificent provider. In many ways, Harry Smith was a wonderful dad.

He was an outgoing guy with a gift for making the ladies laugh. A handsome man with dark skin, a pointed nose, and smiling eyes, Dad was often described as a black Clark Gable. He had a way with people. On Saturday afternoons, men from the neighborhood congregated in our little house on the East

Side as he handed out money while making notations on a writing pad. Only later did I realize that Harry was a loan shark who, early in life, had learned how to make a quarter on a dollar. In a business culture where blacks couldn't borrow money from legitimate institutions, impromptu methods—like Dad's—became commonplace in the community. My natural dad's mother could also wheel and deal. She ran a big numbers business, which was actually an illegal lottery. Grandma had money.

Grandma was also generous. Every couple of months she invited me over to her East Side house to spend the weekend. She took me shopping on Gay Street, where the Bel Air market sold everything imaginable. I loved the excitement of commerce and the strong trust between the Jewish merchants and black customers. Grandma always knew that the butcher gave her his best meat and the green grocer his freshest produce. She'd pick out a chicken and we'd watch as the poultry man wrung the animal's neck. After food shopping, we'd go clothes shopping for me. I was given sweaters, pants, and shoes—as well as advice.

"Don't forget," said Grandma, "that Harry and Jeter have taken you in out of the goodness of their hearts. No one forced them to do it, child. They did it out of love. So you be sure and do everything that's asked of you. You mind them. I'd take care of you myself, but I got Carol May to look after."

Grandma made it plain. Calvin, her son and my blood dad, was a loose cannon. In addition to me, he had fathered Carol May with another woman. Raising the two of us would have been too much for Grandma, whose message to me was *Consider yourself lucky. If you do anything to upset Harry or Jeter, you could be out on the street.* That message sank in and stayed with me for as long as I lived in Baltimore.

Dad made money on his loans, but our financial security came from his salaried job. The city of Baltimore afforded black men few opportunities, but he was able to get full-time work in the sanitation department. Garbagemen had good benefits and decent retirement pay. Dad worked in Jewish neighborhoods where the people often gave him stylish clothing, good appliances, and bottles of the best wine and liquor.

Harry Smith was a loving dad. He wouldn't hesitate to hug me, kiss me, and make it safe for me to tell him whatever little problems were on my mind. Later I realized that his affection was born of his own deprivation. He had never known a caring father. Not once did Dad ever mention his father. I never saw the man myself or heard anyone speak of him. Harry was determined to be the father he never had, and I was the beneficiary of his determination.

I spent a great deal of time with Martha and her mom, Edie, whose sister, the woman I called Aunt Dorothy, was one of the most exciting people I'd ever met. In her silk dress and feather hat, her bouffant hairdo and high heels, she looked like Lena Horne in *Stormy Weather*. She was pure Hollywood. We loved to listen to her stories about her days in New York and her nights in Atlantic City. Then one day she stopped coming around. The reason shocked us: in a fit of jealous rage, her husband had strangled her to death. The mourning went on for months. I remember Edie and Dorothy's mom, Grandma Sarah, wearing a black veil that covered her face. I remember the silence that fell over our neighborhood. I remember being told that if we played at Grandma Sarah's house, we must do so quietly, out of respect for the tragic loss of her beautiful daughter Dorothy.

Jeter, formerly Aunt Dee and now simply Mom, kept me close to her during times of tragedy. She would assure me that while bad people exist, they were far outnumbered by good people. I believed her. She had a bond to the God of love that was powerful and permanent. She was the spiritual rock of our household, a woman who had survived the Great Depression with her soul, optimism, and gratitude intact. At the same time, I detected resentment from Mom that she had felt obliged to care for me. From time to time, she didn't let me forget that I was not a blood relative. The message I got from her was double-edged: The first was *We love you and you're welcome*; the second, *You're here but you're not a full-fledged family member.*

During the day, Mom turned the radio dial to gospel music—Sister Rosetta Tharpe, Willie Mae Ford Smith, Mahalia Jackson, and the CBS Trumpeteers, a Baltimore-based quartet that sang about the "Milky White Way." These were the sounds of a determined people singing messages to excite the spirit and strengthen the heart.

Mom worked as a cook and housekeeper for Jewish families in the more affluent white neighborhoods of East Baltimore. She invariably came home with good reports about her employers. But work, church, and shopping were the only times Mom left the house. Her stutter was so extreme that words locked inside her mouth. At work, she got by because her employers understood and made few verbal demands. If someone rang our bell at home, though, I was the one to open the door. I also always answered the phone. In the presence of Dad and me, Mom was more fluent, but in addressing the outside world, she had a terrible problem making herself understood. As time passed, she became more and more a prisoner of both her stammer and her shame over it.

Shame also shadows same-sex attraction, and yet my first realizations of that phenomenon were free of negative feelings. I thought, for example, that Billy, an overtly feminine man in his early twenties who came through our neighborhood, was a wonder. I related to him completely. He was sharp and quick and clean as a whistle. He wore his hair in the latest process; his outfits were selected with care and flair. His chocolate brown alligators matched his chocolate brown silk shirt. He was graceful as a dancer and smiled like a movie star. When Billy walked down the street, everyone clustered around him. I studied his walk and thought to myself, *That's who I want to be like; that's the way to dress, speak, and move through these streets.*

The other stars were the drum majors who marched in front of the Elks Lodge band. When they showed up, normal life stopped. We ran out of our houses to catch a glimpse. I related to these boys; I knew that they were like me. I loved the flamboyance, the fantastic uniforms, the fur hats, the white boots, the gold batons that they twirled with such theatricality. One time an especially daring drum major threw his baton so high in the air that it stuck in the branches of a tree. Everyone gasped. But just then the wind blew up. It dislodged the baton from the branch and—unbelievably!—it tumbled down into the waiting hand of the drum major, who began twirling it again without missing a beat. The crowd exploded with cheers, as if someone had dropped money out of a plane. That's when I knew that someday I had to be a drum major.

Meanwhile, I fell deeper in love with Karl, who had a decidedly heterosexual demeanor. That wasn't true of Babychild*, another little soft boy like me. He lived at the end of the block. His mom and Arlene were close. I think both mothers sensed that he and I were alike. He had a girlish way about him. Our rapport was magical. We would sit on the stoop next to one another and just watch the people pass by. We didn't have to say a word. Even then, we both knew.

At least on the surface, it seemed that being attracted to other little boys—even to the point of having crushes—was natural. I didn't get any flack—no dirty looks, no reproaches from anyone in my large extended family. I was a romantic child and saw love everywhere I looked. Like most children, I was innocent. That innocence, though, was short-lived. Its violation came early, and the result was unspeakably confusing.

I was no older than three or four. We were still living on the East Side in that connected community of row houses and alleyways where no one owned a car and kids could run around as they liked. If you acted up, a neighbor was just as likely to give you a whipping as your own mama. It was a community that took care of its own.

But no community, no matter how protective of its own, is free from the age-old manipulation and misuse of children. Like untold millions, I was such a child—carefree and happy to be living in this village where a sense of protection was so evident, yet, at the same time, forced into acts that could never be revealed.

It started on a day when I had to go to the store for Mom. On the way back, Dad's brother called me into the house he shared with his mother. I can still remember the smells of that house, the darkness, my feelings of fear. My uncle was a quiet man who had lost a leg in the war. When I walked inside, my uncle was seated alone in the living room. The shades were drawn, and he motioned me to stand in front of him. He exposed his erect penis and told me to touch it. I didn't want to. I wanted to run. But he held me tight and forced his penis into my throat. He held my head so I couldn't move. I couldn't breathe. With everything in me, I struggled for air. Tears streamed from my eyes. I was powerless and horrified. I didn't understand anything. I had never known violence before. When he ejaculated down my throat, I gagged even more. My panic deepened; I was still fighting for air. When he finally released me, he put his finger over his mouth as if to say, *Don't tell anyone*. I was a three-year-old trained to obey adults. Adults protected me, fed me, put me to bed. The concept of going against an adult was forbidden. Yet this adult had just raped me.

Thus began many years of covert encounters. "Mention this to anyone," said my uncle, "and I'll call you a filthy little liar. Tell my brother and I'll come over and slit your throat while you're sleeping."

So it continued for eight more years. At times I thought about telling Dad but, as a child, I reasoned that the revelation would make my mother and father hate me. Besides, it would be my word against Dad's brother's. Dad probably wouldn't believe me, or if he did, he'd say it was my fault. I kept hearing my grandmother's warning: he and Mom, who expressed ambivalence about my living in her house anyway, might even kick me out on the street.

I didn't know what to do, so I did nothing. I simply couldn't tell anyone. Decades later, as an adult, I did speak of it in public. I had become a minister and was preaching a sermon to my congregation. I was talking about how you can go to Christ with everything.

"Give God your truth," I said, "whatever that might be, and let God begin to do a perfect work in you. But don't give God the easy truth. Give God your deepest truth, your deepest secrets, those that have been festering in your heart for years. Maybe even for your entire life. Go to God with your pain, your suffering, and your shame. Let God take that suffering from you and lift that shame off your shoulders. I'm talking about the shame brought on by that uncle or that aunt, that mother or father or teacher or neighbor, that cousin or that preacher who robbed you of your innocence. That person who touched you and confused you with sexual feelings you were too young to understand. Just go to God with it all! Just give it up!"

For the first time, my church exploded. One woman screamed out at the top of her lungs, "All of them! My brother, my uncle, my neighbor, my cousin! Every last one of them!" Within seconds, she was joined by another worshipper, and then another, until the building was shaking with the shouts of dozens upon dozens of people who had been secretly abused at a time in their lives when they were frightened into submission. The screaming went on for fifteen minutes. Some parishioners, overcome with the memory of the pain, passed out. Others couldn't stop crying.

The truth can be overwhelming: everyone's story has a subtext. There are dark secrets, unspeakable events, traumas that cannot be voiced or revealed. Or so the world tells us. Or so we tell ourselves. Even as we are submerged into the baptismal waters, even as we claim new birth in Christ's eternal energy, there are tales that too often remain untold.

As the spirit moved in waves up and down the pews of my church, one believer after another could not contain the pain. My ushers ran out of smelling salts and tissues. I had touched upon the great secret issue of our society.

Years later my sister Martha told me that Dad's brother would also have sex with young girls on the kitchen floor in full view of the other little girls playing in the backyard. He made sure to leave the door open so the kids could watch him. The man was clearly sick.

Today we know something about sexual compulsivity. Back then, it was an untreated disease with no name. Everyone suffered, perpetrator and victim alike. Everyone stayed silent and let the cancer that is shame and self-loathing work its way through the soul.

At the time, I simply endured it. It existed alongside the rest of my life. It was a secret experience that was given no explanation; it had no voice; it stayed stuffed inside, silent and afraid. Outside, I was a girly little boy. I liked jacks. I liked jumping rope, double Dutch, hopscotch, and all the rest. I was comfortable sitting on the stoop and talking to the girls.

I've been asked whether my uncle's molestation shaped my sexuality. Its impact was profound in many ways, but my sexual orientation was there from the start. For example, my crush on Karl with the wavy hair happened before the encounter with my uncle. I was born not only to love other men but also with an inherent longing to be female. As early as I can remember, I would look in the mirror and tuck my penis behind my legs to pretend that I had a vagina.

My desire for sexual reinvention, unlike my homosexuality, has been something I have not broadcast. As someone whose passion was for ministering to my people, I knew that revealing it would only impede my goal.

As an adult, I found the revelation of my mission taking a dramatic turn. I had dreams in which my people were suffering from a horrible sickness long before the literal suffering began. I knew that I had to address that suffering. I was called to do so. The fact that the church remained silent about this suffering made my mission all the more imperative. My vocation was about serving others. To reemerge in the world as a woman would have complicated a vocation I felt compelled to keep simple.

Looking back on my childhood molestation, I do not see it connected to my sexual orientation. As my improbable hit recording from the Golden Age of Disco proclaimed, I was born this way.

At an early age, the excitement of show business also invaded my heart and changed my emotional disposition. The excitement motivated me to become a performer. Back in the forties and fifties, Baltimore blacks could go to only two beaches—Carr's and Sparrow's. The others were off-limits. Carr's was my favorite because, right there by the water's edge, famous rhythm and blues stars performed on a makeshift platform. Sometimes I went there with my half sister Carol May, who was two years younger than me. She wore a white skirt, I wore white trousers, and we both sported white buck shoes. The deejay-emcee was a man named

Hot Rod. He booked all the big acts, including Ray Charles. I got close enough to touch Ray's hand, and when his band took off, I grabbed Carol and we started in on the backwards slop, the dance of the day. (Decades later, Michael Jackson called it the moonwalk.) We tore it up. Everyone stood there, just looking at us and applauding. Ray was playing his raucous "I Got a Woman," and we were rocking so hard that Ray's band members whispered in his ear for him to play the song again. I loved moving to his music and being part of his show, so much so that I was thinking, *If only Ray could see me!* That feeling would stay with me and push my life in a whole different direction.

MOVING WEST

As the forties became the fifties, Baltimore's neighborhoods changed. When the city decided to broaden certain streets on the East Side, Mom and Dad got $2,000 in compensation for our home. With Dad's good job as a garbageman, that was enough for a down payment on a little house on the West Side, where blacks were moving into an area that had been predominantly Jewish.

They bought a lovely little home on Lauretta Avenue from the Krofts. On the way over to see the house, I asked Mom and Dad, "Are they white?"

"No," Mom answered. "They're Jewish."

Negotiations were concluded quickly and amicably, all parties shook hands, and a few weeks later we moved west.

It was still a row house—I never knew anyone in Baltimore who didn't live in a row house—but of higher quality than anything I had seen. Every house on the block, including ours, had a front porch with gliders and pots of blooming flowers. Between the pavement and the front curb were small plots of grass. Instead of old faded marble, the steps were constructed of fancy brick. Dad gave Mom enough money to buy porch furniture and an inflated pool for me in the backyard.

Inside the house we had our first telephone, a party line shared by several families. If the phone rang, I would pick it up to save Mom embarrassment over her stutter. When it came time for furniture shopping, Mom took me along. We selected a dining room table with a pull-out leaf, matching chairs, and a china closet. In the basement was a double sink, a workroom for Dad, and a wind-up RCA Victrola encased in a wooden cabinet. The Krofts had left the old phonograph along with a collection of 78 rpm albums.

God bless the Krofts! Their records were like a hidden treasure, and I spent hours listening to the music of Glenn Miller, Benny Goodman, Paul Whiteman, Kate Smith, and Sophie Tucker singing "My Yiddishe Mama." I'd wind up the phonograph and stand in front of the horn-shaped loudspeaker, drinking in the sweet sounds.

Upstairs in my own room, I slept in a bed with a headboard and Hollywood built-in sliding-door bookcase. Mom made me a gorgeous quilt, and at night I curled up in bed and read Robert Louis Stevenson's *Treasure Island,* my mind drifting off to a world of pirates and buried gold.

My first Christmas on the West Side, I walked down the snow-covered Baltimore streets holding Dad's hand.

"Son," he said, "we're buying the biggest Christmas tree that God ever made."

We arrived at the tree lot and, sure enough, Dad picked up the tallest of the bunch. As we dragged it home, he made me feel as though I were helping pull it along, even though it was his enormous strength that did the job.

When it came to taking care of his family, Dad had an attitude typical of his generation. As soon as he made enough money, he wanted Mom to stop working. Once we moved to the West Side, she became a stay-at-home mom. That meant milk and cookies waiting for me every day after school. As the only child in the household, I had all the attention I wanted.

Looking back, though, I see that the move injured Mom in a

profound way. When she had worked, she'd been forced out of the house; she had to interact with others. Even though her stutter made her reluctant to speak, in work situations she had no choice. But now that Dad had brought us to this higher lifestyle, she could retreat. Shopping could be challenging, but Mom had worked out a way of communicating with the butcher and other merchants. She simply pointed to what she wanted and I did most of the talking. She'd speak with her family, of course, but more and more she cut herself off from the outside world.

Dad was understandably proud of his new status in this classier neighborhood. He was a family man, and now that his family was even better provided for, there was more snap in his step. But family man or not, Saturday changed him into a different person. Saturday night he came home a drunken monster.

Saturday began with me cleaning the house under Mom's close supervision. I scrubbed the upstairs bathroom, polished the hardwood floors in the bedrooms, the staircase, the living and dining rooms. I took down every object from the shelves and painstakingly dusted each one. I mopped the kitchen floor. I hated Saturdays because, while other kids got to play, I was forced to stay inside and scrub. There was a frenetic energy behind this work that came from Mom. Only later did I realize that she took the anxiety she was feeling about Dad's Saturday night escapades and channeled it into cleaning. Every inch of our home had to be spotless. It was as if Jeter were saying to Harry, *How could you hit me? Don't you see that everything here is perfect? How could you come home drunk and beat me?*

It did no good. Harry went out alone. With his tailored mohair suit, white silk shirt, shined-up Stacy Adams shoes, and fine felt Stetson fedora, he disappeared for a good six or seven hours. Saturday night was drinking night, and when Dad came home, he was rip-roaring drunk. This was the moment, of course, that Mom and I had been dreading all day. Liquor made Dad violent.

He'd hit Mom—hard—for no reason at all. Mom cried in pain, but she just endured it. Her cries went through me like a knife. But that's all she did—cry. The next morning, she'd put an extravagant Sunday breakfast on the table. The three of us ate together as though nothing had happened. The previous night's beating was never discussed. This was our family pattern.

I could have easily built up a vicious resentment of Dad. But probably because he was never violent with me, I didn't. Like Mom, I saw him as the provider who had to be respected and served, no matter what. Every night before I went to sleep, I set his plate, fork, and knife for breakfast the next morning and placed a carefully folded linen napkin over the setting to protect it from dust. In many ways, Dad returned my love. Every day when he came home from work, he brought sweets from the Jewish bakery. He got down on all fours and let me ride horsey on his back. If I seemed soft to the more athletically inclined boys in the neighborhood, Dad accepted me the way I was. He gave me a cocker spaniel named Rex, my constant companion. I talked to Rex like he was my sibling. He docilely sat on my lap while I studied the design made by the veins of a leaf or the bark of a tree. I loved nature and its dazzling, ever-changing colors— the pink-orange clouds at sunset, the new green grass in spring, the misty blue of the summer sky. And I told Rex all about it. He'd look at me, wag his tail, and move his head from side to side, as if he understood every word I said.

Dad had Fridays off. That's when he did the shopping at the East Side Bel Air market for his wife and mother. While shopping, he dropped me off at the senior citizen public housing that Grandma Martha shared with her son, Uncle Will. After Dad left, my uncle would pull down the shades and the horrors started all over again.

I kept hoping that Grandma Martha would come out of her room and stop her son, or that someone in that busy neighborhood would wonder why, in the middle of the day, the shades were drawn. I kept praying that someone would knock on the door to make sure everything was all right.

No one ever did. Meanwhile, I had nightmares in which I was chased by a boogeyman looking to kill me. Just as he cornered me, I awoke, filled with terror.

When I came back to Baltimore as an adult, I gained insight into my childhood. Having moved out of the city of my birth years before, I returned for a nostalgic walk through the geography of my childhood. In my old West Side neighborhood, I happened upon Mrs. Jordan, a neighbor I had adored as a child.

"It's Sammy!" she said, calling me by my nickname from back in the day. "You were our favorite little boy because of your singing. We'd wait for your mother to send you on an errand because we knew that would mean you'd be walking through the alleyways singing a song. Oh Lord, Sammy, how we loved hearing you sing! We'd tell each other, 'Here comes Sammy singing!' And somehow we knew that everything was going to be all right."

As she spoke, my childhood came back to me: I saw myself as that little boy—little Sammy—walking from one end of Baltimore to another, singing all the way. I was a singing fool. I couldn't stop if I had wanted to. And it was more than the gospel music I heard on Baltimore radio from the deejay known as Aunt Pauline, whose theme was the Caravans' "Lord, Keep Me Day by Day." Naturally I knew and loved those songs that filled my mother's house. One of the first I memorized was Mahalia Jackson singing about "A Rusty Old Halo." I can still recite the lyrics about a rusty old halo, a skinny white cloud, and a robe so woolly it scratches. Strange, but it was a country and western tune made righteous by the amazing volume of Mahalia's sacred voice.

Even as a child, I had a big booming voice that could be heard everywhere. Joy lived inside me. But the joy born out of music wasn't restricted to gospel. I loved Frankie Lymon, Little Richard, Teresa Brewer, and Etta James. The crazy thing was that I could imitate all those singers. Mesmerized by the chirping birds in our backyard, I imitated their song. I could sing like a bluebird or a sparrow. I would sing along with Patti Page and Tony Bennett. I also loved the movie musicals—the singing and dancing of Donald O'Connor and Debbie Reynolds, Fred Astaire, and Frank Sinatra, Ray Bolger, and Ethel Merman. My favorite films were *Stormy Weather, Cabin in the Sky,* and *Carmen Jones.* I loved the fantastic set designs and fancy costumes worn by Ethel Waters, Lena Horne, and Dorothy Dandridge. Above all, I loved that transformational moment when the speaking voice turned to song.

"I sing because my soul is happy," Mahalia sang in "His Eye Is On the Sparrow," "I sing because I'm free." And Lord knows I was happy and free when I was singing. I had my problems and I had my fears. My uncle snared me into his lair whenever he could. I was a little boy who wanted to be a little girl in a culture that had no place for such feelings. As an only child, I was much loved by my godparents, but I suspect that all only children yearn for a brood of brothers and sisters. I had always been told that my birth mother, Arlene, was a wonderful person and my birth dad, Calvin, whom I practically never saw, was a good guy. But deep in my soul I also knew I had been given away. That is strange and difficult information for a child to grasp.

Meanwhile, life on the West Side went on. Dad brought home baseball mitts and football gear that sat in the basement untouched. I loved the chemistry set he gave me, but I wanted to play with dolls and dress them in matching outfits.

The Warren* family lived two blocks down. Mrs. Warren ran a foster home and was especially accepting of me. They had a son of their own, I'll call him Matthew, with whom I fell madly in love. I was eight, he was eleven, and he became my constant companion. Like me, Matthew was an only child, had a musical soul, and loved to dance. If other boys tried to bully me, Matthew stopped them in their tracks. He made sure no one took advantage of my softness.

Matthew was clearly heterosexual, but that made no difference. As time went on, my feeling for him deepened. I remember a birthday when we kids were in the basement playing spin the bottle. A red lightbulb glowed above our heads. My eyes were on Matthew. As I spun the bottle, I prayed it would point to Matthew. When it landed at the feet of a girl instead, I pretended to enjoy the kiss. I remember that when the other kids left the party and Matthew and I were alone, "Lawdy Miss Clawdy" by Lloyd Price was on the record player. I moved toward Matthew and he moved toward me. I remember that he put his arm around me. He saw me as a girl. That's how I wanted to be seen. There was no sexual contact. Nor did I long for any such contact when I went to bed that night, dreaming of him. I longed only for this boy—for his love, his affection, his eyes gazing into mine. And so it went—my life as a budding homosexual and hopeless romantic.

Romantic love was a powerful part of my young years. But just as powerful was God's love. I felt that love present in both my godparents, even though neither of them took me to church. Mom's stutter kept her home, and Dad had no interest in religious services. Yet a church found me. A church came along and rocked my world, rocked my life, rocked my very soul, and left me transformed. Now, nearly sixty years later, I still remember the excitement and joy of entering the world of the good news.

PROVIDENCE COMES KNOCKING

God is. God is life itself. You possess life; you possess God. God is the source of all life. God is time itself. God is also beyond time. God's love is changeless and, at the same time, causes change. Sometimes that change is announced by a simple knock on the door.

For me, the knock came on a weekday when I was seven. I was doing my homework. Mom was ironing. I went to the door, and a well-dressed black woman was standing there, smiling.

"I'm Mrs. Wood," she said, "and I'd like to speak with your mother."

Mom invited the lady inside. Mrs. Wood explained that her brother-in-law, Reverend Wood, was taking over the ministry of the Providence Baptist Church and that she was recruiting children to attend their Sunday school and participate in their youth activities.

My mother was only too glad to have me join a congregation. And just like that, I entered the world of Reverend Marcus Garvey Wood. And what a world it was! It was, thank the Lord, the world of enlightened African American Christianity at a pivotal moment in our people's history. Reverend Wood had gone to Crozer Theological Seminary in Chester, Pennsylvania, with Martin Luther King Jr. They were close friends. Reverend, who always referred to Martin by his nickname, "Mike," got his master of divinity degree in 1951 and came to Providence in 1952, the year I met him. He presided over the congregation for the next half century. In those early years, when I sat under his teaching, he was immersed in the burgeoning civil rights movement.

Reverend Wood, like Dr. King, had been deeply influenced by his study at Crozer. The school had opened both men's hearts and minds to the possibilities of liberation theology and political activism. Reverend encouraged us not to swallow the Bible whole but to challenge it. We were taught that you can feel God's love while realizing that the Good Book, with its enormous historical, theological, and poetic complexities, can only be read subjectively. Interpretation is unavoidable. *Challenging traditional readings of the Bible and accepting God's grace are not mutually exclusive.*

At Providence Baptist, I was led to feel God's grace. In that church, I felt mystical warmth, an acceptance of who I was. I was a child who wanted to be a member of the hardest-singing gospel group, the Davis Sisters, but I also wanted to be Doris Day. I loved Jimmy Durante, Ray Bolger, Uncle Miltie Berle, and Sid Caesar. I adored everything about Perry Como—his smooth voice, his relaxed style, his cardigan sweaters. I related to *Father Knows Best* and *Leave It to Beaver.* I did not feel alienated from white culture. I did not feel alienated from black culture. I was a child who felt, in the enlightened spirit of Reverend Wood's church, that I belonged to all these worlds. When I opened up my little heart, God stepped in and said, *You are mine.*

It was at the Providence Baptist Church that I was baptized and accepted Jesus Christ. For all the years to come—calm years and crazy years, hurting years and healing years—Christ has remained in my heart.

The wonderful thing about Providence Baptist was this: the church proclaimed the authority of God, but Reverend Wood granted us the right to question authority. He believed in rigorous intellectual investigation. He encouraged free thought. At the same time, he let it be known that the spiritual life was all about the love of Jesus. I felt that love when Reverend said, "Carl, you are loved just as you are. You don't have to learn it or earn it. It's simply there. God loves you because God *is* love. Can't you feel that?"

I could. I still do.

Because I was an eager student with a passion for learning, Reverend placed me in the Jackie Robinson Youth Council of the National Association for the Advancement of Colored People, the largest and most important NAACP chapter in the country, where we were trained in leadership skills. There I came under the influence of Lillie M. Jackson, president of the organization from 1947 until 1970. During my childhood, Miss Lillie was a bold soldier in the battle against segregation, a respected national figure in the movement. She became known as the "Mother of Freedom." Through her pioneering efforts, blacks were admitted to the University of Maryland as well as public pools and parks. Miss Lillie encouraged us to use the library. Thanks to her encouragement, I read Paul Laurence Dunbar and studied the literature and art of the Harlem Renaissance. Miss Lillie spoke to us about the responsibility of learning the history of our people and then helping to shape that history in a positive direction.

In April of 1957, Miss Lillie invited the renowned lawyer Thurgood Marshall to address the Youth Council. In 1954 Marshall had won the landmark *Brown v. Board of Education* case before the Supreme Court, which rejected the myth of "separate but equal" and ended legal segregation in the United States. In 1967, Marshall would become the first African American Supreme Court justice. In his speech, a week before my thirteenth birthday, Marshall told us that a march at the Lincoln Memorial in D.C. was being planned to remind the nation that true integration had yet to be realized. He asked all of us on the Youth Council, "Would you like to join us in Washington for this historic occasion?"

My hand was the first to shoot up.

"Yes!" I declared. "I want to march."

And march we did. On May 17, a chartered bus took us to Washington, where hundreds of similar buses arrived from all over the country. Over 25,000 people attended, the biggest throng I had ever seen. Bayard Rustin had helped organize the demonstration, called the Prayer Pilgrimage for Freedom. Mahalia Jackson sang. Roy Wilkins, Adam Clayton Powell, and A. Philip Randolph spoke. It was also the first time I heard Martin Luther King Jr. speak. The others were brilliant, but Martin was beyond brilliant. He electrified the crowd with what later became known as his "Give Us the Ballot" speech.

"Give us the ballot," he said, "and we will no longer have to worry the federal government about our basic rights.

"Give us the ballot and we will no longer plead to the federal government for passage of an antilynching law; we will, by the power of our vote, write the law on the statute books of the South and bring an end to the dastardly acts of the hooded perpetrators of violence.

"Give us the ballot and we will transform the salient misdeeds of bloodthirsty mobs into the calculated good deeds of orderly citizens. . . .

"Give us the ballot and we will quietly and nonviolently, without rancor or bitterness, implement the Supreme Court's decision of May seventeen, 1954."

Dr. King's "I Have a Dream" speech, delivered in this same spot some six years later, was more famous and drew a far greater crowd. But that earlier speech and that day transformed my life.

Our meetings of the Jackie Robinson Youth Council were

given over to courses in the history of nonviolent protest. In preparation for sit-ins and boycotts, we were trained to resist passively. When our team leaders called us "niggers" and "coons," when they pretended to spit at us and even shoved us to the ground, we learned not to react. We learned the real meaning of "turn the other cheek."

"Our walk with Christ," Reverend Wood reminded us, "isn't simply a walk to church. It isn't simply a walk to the baptismal pool. It's a walk into the world, where real-world problems of justice must be faced. Our walk with Christ takes us into the area that goes beyond good words into good deeds. Christ teaches us how to carry out those deeds with grace, love, and effectiveness. Christ teaches us that love is the most effective tool of all."

When I read the Bible, I identified with Jesus. I saw him as an only child like me. I saw him as hanging out with the outsiders. Because of my same-sex orientation, I saw myself as an outsider who—praise God!—was embraced by a church whose spiritual leader loved outsiders. Jesus himself was an outsider who challenged his elders and questioned religious authorities. Yet his mandate was not to scorn but to love. How could I *not* love this Jesus? How could I *not* see him as my salvation, my savior from a world in which murderous prejudice had led to the enslavement of my people?

There was also the undeniable fact that, at every turn, Jesus went his own way. In a culture of extreme conformity, he blazed his own trail. He didn't answer to any church, prince, or king. He answered only to his divine father. He sought his father's will. He understood that this world's willful ways require righteous scrutiny.

I especially loved the story in Luke's gospel of Jesus and his parents going to Jerusalem to celebrate Passover. After the holiday, on the road back to Nazareth, Mary and Joseph realized that Jesus wasn't there. They turned around and, searching for three days, "found him in the temple courts, sitting among the teachers, listening to them and asking them questions." I was also a child who loved to sit at the feet of my elders like Miss Lillie and Reverend Wood. I marveled when Reverend said, "Just as Jesus was alive in Palestine thousands of years ago, Jesus lives in me today. Jesus is the reconciler, the healer, the forgiver. All teachings of Christ are rooted in forgiveness. The spirit of God transcends blame and guilt. Jesus turns fear into faith."

My faith deepened, and as a preteen I joined the Baptist Training Union that met Sunday evenings at church. This group pursued a serious study of Christianity as a code of moral and social behavior that went beyond simple Bible stories. I was taught that ours is a religion of courage, integrity, and justice.

In public school, I also observed that some of my teachers displayed feminine or soft mannerisms. They didn't accost me or solicit sexual favors—not at all. They were distinguished men whose erudition was a wonder to behold. At the same time, though, in their sensitivity I felt a common bond. I knew they were like me. At church, sexual orientation was not discussed.

Reverend Wood had taken the Providence pulpit from another powerful preacher, Dr. Eugene W. White. I was blessed to hear Dr. White just a few months before he died. In addition to being a preacher who could pierce your heart with the sweet sincerity of his speech, he had a lovely singing voice. He loved to sing "Life Is Like a Mountain Railroad," a song that said, "Life Is Like a Mountain Railroad with an engineer that's brave/We must make the run successful from the cradle to the grave/Watch the curves, the fills, the tunnels, never falter, never quail/Keep your hand upon the throttle and your eye upon the rail." Strange how a simple little tune like that can live inside your soul. During the toughest times in my life, that song, sung in the voice of Dr. White, has come back to comfort me.

At Providence, I became a gleaner, an honor that made me

proud. It meant wearing a white cassock and going up and down the pews with the offering plate. One morning Reverend called me out in front of the entire congregation and said, "We have many wonderful children in our church. They each have great potential. Little Carl Bean, for example, the son of Jeter and Harry Smith, will one day preach. I can say that with assurance because I have heard this young boy express his faith in God. When he speaks of the goodness of the Lord, it's coming from a place in his heart filled with love. Everyone who knows Carl understands what I'm saying. He is articulate beyond his years. He has a bright mind and a spirit that will call him to serve."

I loved hearing Reverend's words, and I believed him. Not long afterward, he sent me to the Virginia Union University for summer seminars where the great Reverend Doctor Samuel DeWitt Proctor, Reverend Wood's cousin and one of the legendary preachers in black Christianity, mentored me. Later, Reverend Proctor succeeded Adam Clayton Powell Jr. as pastor of the Abyssinian Baptist Church in Harlem, where he accepted openly homosexual couples as members of his congregation. Men like Reverend Proctor inspired me to believe that I would preach, I would follow Jesus, I would live in the light of the Lord. What I didn't know, though, was that before that could happen, the world would have its way with me. And as we all know, the world is filled with confusion.

THE HAT

When I was between the ages of nine and fourteen, more than a few older men had their way with me. Some were relatives, some neighbors. They saw me as a soft, chubby boy with round buttocks and full breasts. There was no hiding the fact that I was gay. This excited their aggression.

At age twelve, I was asked by a man and woman to care for their babies while they went to dinner. This was a couple I knew well and trusted implicitly. I was honored that they trusted me to care for their precious children. I was also eager to earn extra spending money. The evening began beautifully. The man and woman were dressed in their Saturday night finery and assured me they'd be home by midnight. "Please feed the kids," said the mother. "Then bathe them and have them in bed by eight." "Of course," I assured her.

I did exactly as I was instructed. Then at nine o'clock I heard the key turn in the door. It was the husband. "Is everything okay?" he asked. "Are the kids asleep?" "Yes," I answered. He went to his bedroom, where I presumed he was retrieving an item he'd forgotten. "Carl," he shouted out to me, "please come here for a minute." I walked down the hallway into his bedroom. That's when he grabbed me. He threw me on the bed and violently pulled my pants and underwear to my knees. His only lubrication was a small amount of saliva. The anal intercourse

CARL BEAN

was excruciatingly painful. It felt as though my body was being ripped apart. The emotional pain was even more horrible. I had another secret rape to hide, another shameful nightmare that could not be spoken or processed.

The paradox was this: I adored many of these men's wives. These were wonderful women who showered me with affection. They never tired of telling me that I was smart, talented, and sweet. Many of these ladies had a spiritual strength that guides me to this day. I was a boy who was surrounded by loving women with whom I had a natural and remarkable rapport.

I could never relax because of the many men who forced themselves on me. I was their target, their pincushion. I was always on guard. I tried to avoid them whenever I could, but because their wives and I were so close, I often found myself in their homes. When they could get me alone, the men used me sexually. They did so without hesitation or apology. They knew I was too frightened to tell anyone.

In all my growing-up years, in all my intimate discussions with the women I loved so dearly, only one spoke openly of the danger I faced. When I was seven or eight, my natural dad's mom, the one with the lucrative numbers business, said, "Stay away from certain men in our family. If you're alone in a room and they come in, run out." And then she named names. Whenever I could, I heeded Grandma's warning. As it turned out, though, the number of men was far greater than even she had imagined.

As a child, I was loved and abused, indulged and traumatized. Two trains ran on two different tracks. No one benefited more from the presence of wise, warm, and affectionate women. No one was more frightened of predatory men. Yet, in spite of all this, I found a degree of comfort in my domestic routine.

Each day after school, Mom's homemade cookies and fresh milk were waiting for me. When I was through, Mom left the house and walked to the market. That's when I went to her bedroom and took down a hatbox from her top shelf. To reach it, I had to move a chair to the closet, climb up, stand on tiptoes, and grab the box. It's a wonder I never fell and broke my neck. But I was determined, and I was careful, and I never came down off the chair without that hatbox cradled in my arms.

I already loved women's hats and studied them in the movies. Whether Bette Davis or Greta Garbo, the great stars wore fabulous hats. In the musical world, I took careful note of the ostrich-plume-feathered hats worn by the Andrews Sisters and Lena Horne. By any measure, Mom's hat was nothing short of spectacular.

I sat at Mom's vanity table in front of the mirror. The vanity, in the art deco style, was a beautiful shade of light wood. Set before me was an array of perfumes, like Gardenia and Evening in Paris, in crystal bottles with puffy atomizer bulbs. I'd spray myself and apply a small amount of dusting powder. The culmination of my ritual was, of course, removing the hat from the box and placing it on my head. It was black, with a stingy brim and slate gray feather in front. Finally I pulled the hat's delicate veil over my face. I sat there and stared, simply drinking in the moment of bliss.

Dad had hats, shirts, ties, shoes, and boots. But none of his apparel interested me. It was Mom's hat that I loved. Once placed upon my head, it excited my imagination and thrilled my little soul. Yet even as my heart sought solace in things feminine, the church pulled me into things sacred. And because of the strong feminine demeanor of the male singers and musicians in many churches, those two forces did not seem contradictory. A young boy like me was given the idea that gayness in men—especially those in the musical arts—was a fact of life.

Providence Baptist was populated largely by people we called strivers, those looking to advance themselves in not only the intellectual and spiritual realm but the economic as well. These were upwardly mobile Negroes eager to get their fair share of the American dream. The burning issue of the day was social and political equality, not sexual orientation.

In secular Baltimore, I continued to follow the drum majors, a major source of excitement. The big star was a boy named Roy*, who led the Junior Elks band. Roy had style, pride, and a cocky confidence that appealed to the performer who lived inside me. Whenever there was a parade, folks would gather around and start to shout, "Here comes Roy! Roy is out front!" Roy was a star.

I wanted to be Roy. I practiced moves in the backyard for hours on end. I vowed that one day I would become a drum major myself. More than the baton, though, what I wanted was a pair of white drum majorette boots decorated with big tassels. I begged Mom to buy me a pair.

"They're for girls," she said.

"I know, but I'm sure we can find a pair to fit me," I argued.

"Sweetheart," said Mom, who surely knew my true nature and yet pretended otherwise, "why in the world would you want girls' boots?"

"I don't want them," I said. "I *need* them. I can't live without them."

Mom laughed away my request, but I was serious. When I closed my eyes and imagined how those boots would look on me, I'd break out in a smile. The possibility of wearing a complete majorette outfit—the short skirt, the sparkly blouse, and those adorable boots—was heaven on earth.

Another heavenly thought was a boy; I'll call him Ralph. We met when we were preteens and became friends for life. Ralph had dark skin and burning brown eyes. He was cute as a button—and also a year older than me. Compared to me, he was sophisticated. For example, my church experience was limited to Providence Baptist, where the music tended to be "proper" rather than rootsy, but Ralph knew all the storefront Holy Ghost congregations. He was also a superb singer who taught me harmony and schooled me in the nuances of full-throated gospel singing.

Ralph led me in the direction of a new world. That world was gospel and gay, a subculture where artists, many of whom were extravagantly talented, were also flamboyant. At the same time, when I attended those storefront churches at night, I heard my first antigay sermons. Preachers were saying, "Sex between two men is a sin. Sex between two women is a sin. That kind of sex doesn't please God. That kind of sex is wrong. These people are an abomination."

Yet many of those preachers, winking and blinking, were hitting on the gay boys in the choir. The hypocrisy was blatant. I was excited by the music but confused by the church culture that endorsed the music.

"Let's hook school," said Ralph one day.

"And do what?" I asked.

"You'll see. You'll love it."

We walked a good mile, singing Sam Cooke and the Soul Stirrers songs on the way, before Ralph stopped at the front of a row house on a nondescript block.

"Who lives here?"

"A famous queen," said Ralph. "Everyone loves him. Everyone comes here to party."

When he opened the door, the queen was in his house robe. He smiled at Ralph and seemed extremely pleased to see him. On his 45 record player, rhythm and blues, the music Mom forbade, was blasting: Ruth Brown singing, "Mama, He Treats Your Daughter Mean," the Midnighters talking about "Annie Had a Baby." His living room was decorated in green and gold with ornate armchairs and a couch of red velvet. On the walls were paintings of peacocks and portraits of exquisite men. The room was crowded with many boys I recognized from gospel groups around the city. But there were also boys I had never seen before.

"Those are the bad boys," Ralph whispered in my ear. "They just got out of the juvenile home."

The fact that they were far older than we were—eighteen or nineteen—gave them an exotic edge. And their association with criminal behavior made that edge sharper. For the first time, I saw boys sniffing glue and two boys dancing together. Naturally the sight intrigued me. After some initial and awkward conversations, one of the bad boys told me he wanted to take me upstairs. At first, I was hesitant, but I saw that Ralph had also received an invitation from an older guy. The four of us climbed the stairs and went into the queen's bedroom. Some boys were already fooling around on the bed, so they mounted and penetrated Ralph and me on the floor. We did not resist. The experience was quick, cold, and without a second of emotional intimacy. After satisfying themselves, the older guys simply got up and left.

Ralph looked at me and I looked at him. We didn't smile. We didn't laugh. We didn't say a word. We read the pain in each other's eyes. We saw each other's confusion. In some part of our minds, we felt older. We had experienced a rite of passage that, in this culture of bad-boy homosexuality, was terribly important. We had been had. We had allowed ourselves to be had. In some way, we had even invited the experience. But it was without love or a hint of concern. All Ralph and I could do was move closer to one another. He put his arm around me and, for several long and beautiful moments, held me close to his chest.

We were friends, soon to be lovers, who were moving quickly into a world where same-sex relationships grew more and more complex.

———

In the world of drum and bugle corps, I sometimes performed as a drum major. Having mastered the art of baton twirling, I attained a certain status. Even there, though, a sexual subtext was in play. Certain "straight" men became our fans. After observing us, they would often pursue us. This led to a number of encounters.

Why was I so compliant? Surely that has to do with my feminine nature as well as the home in which my godparents raised me. I saw that my loving mother was submissive to her man. After her Saturday night beatings, she cooked him eggs on Sunday morning. She never complained. When I questioned her about Dad's violence, she said, "That's how men are, baby. That's how they're made."

One Saturday night when my birth mother, Arlene, brought me money, she arrived at the very moment that Dad was beating Mom. Arlene was crazy about Jeter—everyone was—and she begged him to stop. Dad's response was to beat her as well. I was amazed to see that Arlene, like Mom, endured it without resistance.

Around that same time, people in our neighborhood were listening to a Billie Holiday record called "'Tain't Nobody's Business If I Do." The lyrics said, "I'd rather my man would up and hit me/Then for him to jump up and quit me . . . I swear I won't call no copper/If I get beat up by my poppa." Billie's tone was defiant, bittersweet, and sad. Those words explained why Mom would take Dad's beating. That's what women did back then—especially southern church gals brought up to submit. But Arlene, my natural mother, hadn't been Dad's woman. Or had she?

My godsister Martha and I were convinced that we were blood relatives. But how could that be? We had different mothers. We had different fathers. Or did we? Harry openly admitted that he had fathered Martha. But what if Harry had also fathered me? What if Harry had gotten Arlene pregnant when she was fourteen? Wouldn't that explain why Harry had been so eager to adopt me and raise me as his own?

These were questions that haunted me. I wanted to ask Mom or Dad, Arlene or any of the relatives in our family, but I didn't dare. I kept the uncertainty inside. Along with Mom's willingness to get along and go along with her husband's erratic behavior, she displayed erratic behavior of her own—at least toward me. I noticed it when one of her nephews came to spend the weekend. He was three years younger than me. She openly favored him in ways designed to remind me that he was a blood relative and I was not. For example, I could never refuse any food served by Mom. He could. He could say, "I don't want green beans. I want potatoes," and Mom would give him potatoes. I wouldn't dare say such a thing. My godparents had raised me never to question but to accept with gratitude. At bedtime, her nephew could say, "I'm not tired, I want to stay up late," and permission would be granted. I couldn't ask that question, knowing in advance that the answer would be a firm no. Mom cared for me, no doubt, but she treated her nephew with such warmth and willing indulgence that I felt "less than."

It's now understandable to me that as a witness to Mom's abuse, I received Mom's scorn. She couldn't express anger at Dad, and so she passively/aggressively directed that anger at me, the only other member of the household. Mom also resented how her husband spoke to me with greater frequency and, oddly enough, with more respect than he showed when he spoke to her. Add in her stutter, another reason she felt so isolated, and you can understand her deep frustration. The impact of Mom's unhappiness on me was painful; I was unable to retaliate or discuss what was happening with a single soul, not even my blood mother. It was something I had to absorb.

The contradictions remained. Despite everything, Mom loved me dearly. Dad always demonstrated tender concern for me. He refused to attend church yet never denigrated religion. When I began going to Providence Baptist, he had no objections. He was pleased to see me reading the Bible and learning about Christ.

After my third or fourth year at church, Dad could see the changes in me. I was filled with energy to do God's work, especially in the area of civil rights. I spoke about justice all the time. I pointed out how Christ himself was a nonviolent man who lived in a violent time and made a difference by showing love for everyone. Dad took notice of what I was saying and the books I was reading, but not until one rainy Sunday morning in April did he ask me a direct question.

"What did Reverend preach on today?"

"The story of the prodigal son," I said.

"I don't know that story. Tell it to me."

I narrated the parable found in Luke about the son who rebels and leaves the father. He's filled with pride and bitterness. On his own, he loses his money and winds up destitute. When he comes home, he must face his failure. He admits his unworthiness. But instead of scorning his son, the father embraces him. The father's love is unconditional. The father and son are reconciled.

After I told the story, Dad looked at me. Something in his eyes told me I had reached him. I didn't push it, though. I just left him alone. A week passed.

Sunday morning. I was getting dressed for church when Dad came into my bedroom.

"Mind if I go with you this morning?" he asked.

"I'd love that," I said.

We went to church together. Dad sat and listened to Reverend's sermon. Dad closed his eyes during the prayer. He held my hand during the final blessing. Hand in hand, we walked out together into the light of early afternoon.

"Well?" I asked. "What do you think of Providence?"

"I think I'll go back next week."

And so he did. Fact is, Dad went to church for the rest of his life. From that day on, he never came home drunk or hit Mom again.

But deliverance, as I later learned, is a sometime thing. You can embrace it today and shrug it off tomorrow. And even though I loved having a daddy who was no longer drinking, there were other things I learned about the man that disturbed me deeply.

At age eleven, I confided in my sister Martha. I had told her, before anyone else, that I was attracted to boys. At fifteen, when she became pregnant, I was the first to know. She named her first child Carla, after me and her husband, Carlos. Her own mother was not nearly as supportive as her stepmom—my mom Jeter. Jeter became the loving, supportive mother Martha always wanted to have. The two were extremely close.

"She's the greatest woman I've ever known," Martha said about Jeter. "She's an angel."

"Dad's wonderful too," I said.

Martha stayed silent.

"Don't you think Dad's a great provider?" I asked, wanting my sister to agree with me.

More silence.

"You don't think Dad's a great guy, Martha?"

"I'm not saying anything."

"Well, I want you to say something," I said. "I want to know how you feel."

"You'll be sorry you asked."

"No, I won't. The truth's the truth."

"You want the truth, Carl? Okay, here's the truth. Ever since Carlos and I moved into our own place, Dad's been borrowing the key."

"What for?"

"Oh, come on, baby bro. You know what for. His women.

While I'm out working, Dad's sneaking his women over there. It kills me to know that he's cheating in my very own bed. It hurts my heart so bad to have to keep this secret from Dee."

The news took my breath away. The shock shut me down emotionally. I didn't want to deal with this revelation; I tried simply to numb the pain. I knew that when I went home to Mom and Dad, I'd have to make sure that our family dynamic remained unchanged. I couldn't betray Dad, and I couldn't hurt Mom.

Another secret encounter rocked my world. This one involved my natural father. I'd see him from time to time when I went to visit Grandma, his mother who was Jeter's sister-in-law as well as Jeter's closest friend. After Nana passed, Grandma became another key maternal figure in my life.

One day Grandma was out shopping and I was downstairs reading. I looked up and there was my father, standing in front of me. He was fidgety and nervous. Seeing me, his son, always put him on edge. Maybe it was because he had never been part of my upbringing, or maybe he didn't want to be reminded of a responsibility he couldn't meet. Whatever the reason, he was usually distant. Today he wasn't. Today he was a little drunk.

"What are you doing?" he asked.

"Just reading," I said.

"What have you been up to?"

"Not much," I answered.

"You fool around with the girls?"

"No," I said.

"I hear you fool around with the boys."

I didn't say anything.

He said it again. "I hear you fool around with the boys."

I still didn't say anything.

"I know you do," he said, his voice turning harsh. "Now get

up those stairs, go in the bedroom, and shut the door behind you."

I hesitated, but when he picked up his arm to strike me, I ran up the stairs and went into the bedroom. A few minutes later he opened the door and walked in. Through his pants, I could see his penis was erect.

I thought to myself, *Lord, have mercy! My father—my own blood father—is gonna force me into sex with him!* I wanted to run, I wanted to hide, but there was no escaping. And just when it was going to happen, when he reached out to touch me, a loud booming noise from the street distracted him. Maybe he thought it was his mother coming home. In any event, instead of touching me sexually, he hauled off and whacked me across the face, as if I had done something to *him*! Then he opened the door and told me to get out. I had another secret that I couldn't tell another living soul.

Secrets. They excite and consume us; they confuse and defeat us. When they remain hidden—unspoken and disguised in darkness—they do the most damage. They overwhelm our minds and corrode our souls. They lead to guilt and self-doubt. They blind us to clarity and distort our sense of reality. They destroy.

Matthew and I had a secret. He was a butch boy who liked girls. I was a chubby boy built like a girl. I knew that Matthew viewed me not only as a friend but as an object of voluptuousness. We openly flirted with one another. He let me know, by his facial and verbal expressions, that he liked my breasts, big backside, and wide hips. I was his secret girlfriend.

It didn't occur to me that either of his parents had any inkling of our secret. After all, they treated me like a second son. I loved spending time in their home. Although without pretensions, Matthew's mom carried herself with a certain confidence typical of educated black women of light complexion. His dad loved music and had a worldly demeanor. He and his charming wife considered me a bright boy and encouraged my friendship with their son. One time at the start of a delicious crab cake dinner, Matthew's dad, much to my amazement, offered me a cold beer.

"My mom would kill me," I said.

"Don't worry, Carl, just take a couple of sips. It makes the crab cakes taste even better."

He poured the beer into a frosted mug. This was the most sophisticated thing I had seen in my twelve years of life. I had never tasted beer before. I didn't love the beer, but I did love the combination of an ice-cold drink with crab cakes.

On another evening, I came by to see Matthew, only to learn that he and his mom had gone shopping. Matthew's dad invited me in.

"Carl," he said. "I'm in the basement. Come on down."

When I went downstairs, he was listening to classical music. I loved what I heard. The soaring strings transported me to another realm. The melodies were both complicated and simple. When Matthew's dad explained the essential elements of a symphony, I was thrilled to have this new musical understanding.

I was also puzzled, though, when he got up, walked upstairs, and locked the door. When he returned, he sat next to me on the couch and, while Beethoven was still blasting, put his arm around me. I moved away.

"Don't be afraid," he said. "Let's just do what you and Matthew do."

My heart dropped. I didn't know what to say or do. I didn't want him to touch me. It seemed wrong in every way. I was repulsed, but I was also wildly confused. How did he know that sometimes Matthew and I had sex? But I let the man have his way. As he penetrated me, I stared into space, my mind lost in a void of dark submission.

"This is just between us," he said, after he ejaculated. "No one can ever know."

I didn't sleep that night at all. One more secret. And one more instance where I saw that lines separating gay and straight often disappear. These lines are not only crossed in prison or military confinement. They're crossed every day under ordinary circumstances. This is why I know for a fact that people don't fit into neat boxes. Sexual categories can be artificial. My early sexual experiences were almost exclusively with heterosexual men. That's when I learned sexual aggression has more to do with power than with sexual orientation.

THE FIRST DAY

Junior high seemed like a big step. I'd be going to school with older kids. I was also excited that ours was to be the first integrated class. Given my involvement with the Jackie Robinson Youth Council, I understood the importance of what was happening. I was part of history. The state-sanctioned exclusion of my people had been challenged and defeated. Separate but equal was exposed as a lie. And I was on the front lines of the battle, a member in good standing of the first integrated class my city had known.

Mom had bought me a new outfit—a yellow and white shirt of fine cotton, chocolate brown trousers with a sharp crease, and penny loafers. I felt good in my clothes but entered the school building with trepidation. Fortunately there were no overt incidents. Some of the white kids were standoffish; others wouldn't even look at us. That was okay. We knew we had every right to be there. We walked proud. If there were uncomfortable moments and occasional scorn, we could take it. We were prepared.

It was a warm September day, and during lunch we black kids walked over to the schoolyard for recreation. That's when we were attacked. Out of nowhere, hoodlums on motorcycles roared through, swinging bats and chains. They swung at our heads, our necks, our chests, our legs—anywhere they could. They came at us screaming at the top of their lungs:

"Kill the niggers!"

"Kill the coons!"
"Go back to your own neighborhood!"
"Go back to the zoo!"

All we could do was run. The school provided no protection. The teachers were nowhere to be found. We were fast and made a mad dash out of the yard and down the street, but several of my classmates tripped and, when they fell, were beaten. Some got their heads smashed in. I was lucky enough to keep my footing and escape. A block away from school a Jewish man saw what was happening and opened his garage to let us in. Then he stood in front of the door, defying the knuckleheads. He let us stay there until it was safe to leave. When I arrived home, my shirt was torn and I had lost two schoolbooks during the chase. I explained what had happened.

"Boy," said Dad, "you're going to have to come up with a better excuse than that. Go to your room and stay there."

I tried to argue, but Dad was in no mood to be questioned.

At a little after six, my mom shouted, "Carl, come down here. Your dad needs to talk to you."

What now? I thought to myself.

"Okay, Harry," Mom addressed Dad. "Please tell Carl what you need to say."

"I'm sorry, son," he said.

My father had never apologized to me before—not for anything. "I just watched the evening news," he went on to say, "and they reported a race riot at your school. Everything you said was true. I'm just glad you weren't hurt. Now tell me exactly what happened."

Dad listened attentively as I narrated the drama. I could see in Mom's worried eyes that she was afraid for me.

"I don't want him going back to that school, Harry," she said.

Part of me agreed with Mom. If school meant enduring crazy hoodlums, I wanted nothing to do with it. But another part of me—the part dedicated to the civil rights struggle—understood that social change required courage. I tried to muster it up, but it wasn't easy. I half hoped that Mom would win the argument with Dad.

"There is no argument," said Dad. "Carl has as much right to attend that school as anyone. So that's where he's going."

And that's where I went.

The experience, at least for the most part, turned out positive. I matriculated with kids of all kinds—Jewish, Catholic, Baptist, and Presbyterian. This was the first time in my young life that I interacted with whites. I liked school and excelled in math. Miss Paulette, my algebra teacher, who was white, gave me all As and let me help mark other students' papers. Sometimes she even drove me back home after school. I made a close friend named Bob*, a Dutch boy who had been raised a Quaker. We talked all the time, but a white friend of his resented our relationship. When the boy called me "nigger," Bob struck him in the face and bloodied his nose.

At the end of the semester, class pictures were taken by a professional photographer—another first for me. That morning I dressed in my Sunday best. But when it was time to go to the auditorium and line up before the camera, the black kids were told to stay in class.

"Why?" I asked Miss Paulette.

"There is no 'why,'" she admitted. "I'm afraid it's just that our principal doesn't want any of the Negro children photographed. The white parents also protested. I think that's terribly unfair, and I've told her so. At the proper time, I intend to protest her decision in front of the school board. For the time being, though, there is nothing we can do."

When I think back, it was extraordinary how Miss Paulette mitigated what otherwise would have been the bleakest of moments. I could easily have turned against white people, but this white woman, blind to color and free of prejudice, kept me from narrow-mindedness and glib generalizations. She was as angry at the principal as I was.

Outside school, I had part-time jobs. Mom and Dad had given me a strong work ethic. I earned money sweeping the floor at a pharmacy owned by Dr. Dickman. When new shipments came in, I helped stock the store.

One Saturday afternoon I was doing exactly that when Dad stopped by to pick up a prescription and wanted to know where I was.

"Oh, he's out back, Mr. Smith," said Dr. Dickman. "He's helping unload a truck that just came in."

Dad came to the back alley and saw what I was doing.

"Stop!" he shouted. "I'm taking you home with me right now!"

I didn't know what was happening. Had I done something wrong?

Next thing I knew Dad was face to face with Dr. Dickman.

"What are you doing," Dad said, "giving a young boy this kind of heavy labor?"

"That's okay, Dad," I said. "I can handle it."

"Quiet, boy!" Dad yelled. "I wasn't talking to you. I was talking to Dr. Dickman."

"Those cartons aren't all that heavy, Mr. Smith. Besides, Carl seems to enjoy the work."

"The work is over," Dad shot back, "and Carl's coming home with me. Right now."

Later that night when I told Mom what had happened, she explained the underlying motive behind Dad's behavior.

"Harry Smith is a proud man," she said, "and doesn't want to see a son of his do what he was forced to do. Before he found work with the city, he had to take jobs loading and unloading trucks. The men he worked for disrespected him. They cheated him out of money and treated him like a slave. So when he saw you lifting heavy boxes at the store, those memories came rushing back."

Every night my father sat and read the paper after work. He often read the more interesting stories out loud while Mom prepared dinner and I set the table.

One evening, Dad was in his easy chair perusing an article in the *Baltimore Sun*'s Sunday magazine. I was sitting on a stool by Dad's feet when he started discussing the story. I remember that the tone of his voice was especially kind, as if he were trying to tell me something but didn't know how.

"Ever hear of someone called Christine Jorgensen, Carl?" he asked.

"No," I said.

"Well, she's an interesting person. She's an American who used to be called George. Then she goes over to Denmark where a doctor turns her into a woman named Christine."

"I don't understand, Dad."

"I don't either. It's the damnest thing I ever read. Here, come take a look."

The article included a picture revealing a pretty lady. She had curly hair, dangling earrings, and smiling eyes. She looked like a regular woman.

"She was in the army with other guys," Dad said. "Then when he gets out, he says he isn't happy being a guy. Wants to be a girl. Now ain't that something?"

He didn't ask the question aggressively or judgmentally. He asked it with sympathy. On several occasions, when both he and Mom had caught me trying on Mom's hat, they laughed and seemed amused. I took it as tacit approval.

Dad wasn't angered or repulsed by Christine Jorgensen. He was simply curious. He gave me the magazine article, sensing that I would cherish it. I kept it in my room for years, often going back to that picture of the pretty lady. I studied her closely to see if there were any signs of her former self as a man. None were apparent. She looked normal and happy. I wondered if, like me, she had tucked in her penis when she was a boy and pretended to have a vagina. I wondered whether there were more people like me and Christine—boys unhappy being boys; boys who acted like girls; boys who, in their heart of hearts, felt like girls. I wondered if I'd ever get to meet someone like Christine and ask her all the questions running through my brain. These thoughts remained unspoken. Many decades would pass before they could be expressed, and even then they would be voiced only in front of my most understanding and compassionate friends.

The passage from childhood to early adolescence is often tricky and fraught with pain. My passage was both. The same great spirit that dwells within every soul dwelt within me. Every day I felt that spirit. The joy of Jesus was always there. I awoke singing, spent my day singing, and went to sleep singing. At school, I excelled alongside the smartest kids. I had close friends. A pattern had emerged, one that had me sexually active with a number of older boys, yet I was able to realize those submissions without losing my cheerful demeanor—at least on the outside. Romantically, I was always connected to one person at a time. But the sexual energy and inquisitiveness that come with adolescence led to experimentation. As in most teens, my hormones were going crazy.

I was known in my neighborhood as a kid with promise. My relationships at school were good. My strong connections at church were based on a common passion for Christ. My friends and mentors at the Jackie Robinson Youth Council were brilliant. Junior high would soon lead to high school and high school would surely lead to college. All my instructors said so. I might become a preacher or a singer, a teacher or a writer. Miss Paulette predicted that I would become a mathematician. Life would proceed in orderly fashion. When once or twice a month my uncle forced me to have sex with him, I did so. A minute later, I blocked it out of my mind.

I was going somewhere. I had been blessed to be adopted by people who had raised my standard of living and looked after me with great love. God was protecting me. God would always protect me. I thought I was safe from harm. But harm came suddenly and with a vengeance that made me forget everything—all my blessings, my education, my dear friends, my kind teachers. In a moment of panic that would redefine my life from that point forward, I tried to kill myself.

BREAKDOWN OR BREAKTHROUGH?

Things started out beautifully. I was fourteen and in the tenth grade at City College, the predominantly Jewish progressive high school. Classes were among the most accelerated of any public school in the country, so when I finished high school, I could skip my freshman year and enter college as a sophomore. I thrived in the intense environment. I adopted the dress code of the other guys—the Brooks Brothers shirts, tennis sweaters, and cordovan shoes. Reverend Wood's son Marcus, who was a year older than me and attended City College, had told me about it. He raved about their music curriculum. He had received formal instruction since he was a small child and read and wrote music fluently.

"You'll do great at City," said Marcus. "You have natural talent."

I might have had talent, but I lacked training.

"No worries, Carl," he said. "You can sing. You sing better than anyone."

I was singing in choirs all over the city at that point, but I sang by ear. In my head, I could hear the sounds that I wanted to make and—praise God—could make those sounds effortlessly. I could sing a Negro spiritual one moment and do a pitch-perfect imitation of Ethel Merman the next. But when it came to sight-reading, I was lost. When I learned that City's music program required an audition, I was petrified.

"I'll never make it," I told Marcus. "When I go in there, they'll give me a piece of paper with notes written all over it and I won't know what to do."

"When you go in there, Carl, have something prepared. Go in with the song you want to sing."

I took Marcus's advice. Mrs. Smith, our choir director at church, had taught me diaphragmatic breathing. I had range—I could go from high tenor to low bass—and I had an innate sense of phrasing. Mrs. Smith also stressed singing from the heart. I knew singing was all about telling a story. The story I chose for my audition came from my own people. It was a spiritual called "Ain't That Good News."

I went to the audition filled with fear. When I was presented with a piece of music, I politely asked whether I could interpret a song of my own choosing. The examiners were surprised but they agreed. The second I started singing, my fear fled. I closed my eyes and let God do the rest. When I was through, the teachers stood and applauded. One gentleman had tears in his eyes.

"Welcome to City College," he said.

Thank God for Mrs. Smith, whose training got me through.

At school, I met a large contingent of gay Jewish boys. This widened my view of homosexuality. I was learning that gay orientation was hardly restricted to blacks. The boys were members of the cheering squad, and it wasn't long before I too became a cheerleader. I could jump and shout with the best of them. Scholastically, I responded well to challenging classes. As a voice major, I could see myself racing through three years of high school and going straight to music conservatory, either Peabody in Baltimore or Juilliard in New York.

Outside school, as one of the flashiest drum majors in the city, I led the Elks Lodge marching band. I was stepping high. I was motivated. I was going places. Nothing could go wrong. And then, at age fourteen, everything did.

I came home one day after school to find both my godparents waiting for me in the living room. Dad's eyes were frozen cold. Mom was crying. She stood several steps behind Dad. Something was terribly wrong.

"Come here, boy," Dad furiously demanded. "Stand in front of me and look me in the eye."

He mentioned a family down the block who had a boy a little older than me. He said the boy's parents had come to him with a story about me. Their boy claimed that I had been sexual with him. The story was true. The boy had been more than willing. In fact, he had been the instigator.

"I told the man that it couldn't be true," said Dad. "Not my Carl. Not my son. Now I want you—in front of your mother and God Almighty—I want you to swear to me that this man is lying. I want to know that his son is lying. I want to hear you say that nothing like that ever happened."

My heart was beating like crazy. A big part of me yearned to tell Dad what he wanted to hear. But that would have been a lie. And the boy, who was telling the truth, would be punished. My conscience couldn't handle that. I didn't want to say the words, but swept up in the emotional moment, I had to.

"It's true," I said.

Mom let out a cry. Dad's eyes turned blood red. "You're saying that you fooled around with that boy. Is that what you're saying?"

"Yes."

The second the word *yes* came out of my mouth, Dad hauled back and whacked me across the face. The blow was powerful enough to knock me to the floor. The pain was far more than physical. My father had never struck me before. Not once.

I started screaming, "Why did you hit me? Why are you angry? Don't you know that all I did was what your own brother has been doing to me since I was a little boy?"

"Shut up!" Dad shouted.

"I won't shut up, I'll never shut up, I'll tell everyone the truth. You've always told me to tell the truth; well, now I'm telling it. I'm going to scream from the rooftops that your brother made me have sex with him for as long as I can remember. Your own brother, sitting in that room with the shades pulled closed. Not only with me, but with girls too. He'll do it with anyone, and he said if I ever told anyone, he'd kill me."

By now I had managed to get up on my feet, but Dad smacked me again, this time even harder. I fell to the floor, but when I got up, I was through talking. With my heart racing even faster, I ran upstairs, screaming, *"I hate you, I hate you, I hate you!"* Mom called after me, but I ignored her. I didn't want to hear her. Didn't want to hear what she or Dad or anyone in the world had to say. I'd been struck, I'd been wounded, my very soul was bleeding. Mom and Dad no longer loved me. They despised me.

I had always been the golden boy. I had appeared on TV singing with glee clubs. The neighborhood women pampered me. My teachers favored me. I was a star at church. I was praised by Reverend and got all As in Bible class. And now this beating, this awful rejection. Everything I had long feared was coming true: Jeter, who half resented being forced to care for me, a non-relative, was throwing me out; Dad, a volatile man, was turning violent toward me.

I knew that Jeter and Harry felt socially inferior to the couple that had told on me. The woman was a licensed vocational nurse. The man had a good job and was a church deacon. And now my parents were faced with accusations that their son was a sissy. A queer. A freak. Well, I wanted them to defend me. I wanted them to say that I was what I was and that was okay with them. I wanted them to say that they loved me and that I was a good boy. I wanted them to say that I had a nature of my own, and that there was nothing wrong with it. But instead I was smacked and cursed and made to feel like a criminal. I felt trapped. I had nothing to say, nowhere to go. I no longer wanted to live. So I locked myself in the bathroom. My head still spinning as if I were drunk, I opened the cabinet and reached for jars of pills. I didn't care what kind of pills. I was going to swallow them all and die. That's all I wanted to do.

One pill jar after another. I emptied them all. Choking and coughing, I managed to get them all down. Drinking and swallowing, crying out words I didn't even understand, I fell to the floor and screamed and cried until I was sucked down into the black void I had sought, my mind finally relieved of thought, relieved of pain and consciousness, a fourteen-year-old boy no longer able to move.

As I gradually came awake, I didn't know where I was. When I moved my left arm, it felt heavy. When I moved my right arm, it felt even heavier. My eyelids felt heavy and so did the weight of my head. My head throbbed, my throat was parched. I wondered whether I was inside a dream. For a while I clung to the notion that I had arrived in a different realm and fantasized about being free of my body. Soon I realized that I was in some sort of a hospital bed. I remembered leaving the house in an ambulance and asking that Dad, despite all that happened, ride with me. He did, but now he was gone.

"Where am I?" I asked.

"You're in the emergency room," said a woman. "I'm the head nurse of the psychiatric ward."

"Am I crazy?"

"You don't look crazy to me. Besides, I got two ladies waiting to see you who tell me you're the smartest boy in town. They say you can sing too."

I didn't understand what the nurse was talking about until I saw my birth mother, Arlene, and her sister walking toward my bed. It was hard to believe, but there they were. Just then I remembered that Mama and Aunt Rosalie worked as custodians in this very hospital. They both leaned over and kissed me.

"Son," said Mama, "don't worry about a thing. They pumped all those pills out of your stomach, and you're going to be just fine. When I found out what happened to you, I went and talked to the doctors over here. They agreed to treat you, and believe me, son, they're the best. We're all family here, and we're going to take real good care of you."

It was bizarre, it was confusing, but it was also wonderful. Through a botched attempt on my life, I had landed in the arms of my natural mother, who sat on the side of my bed, stroking my forehead and whispering words of comfort.

"When it comes to liking boys," said my mother, who'd been going to a gay hairdresser for years, "you ain't the first and you won't be the last guy in our family. Just hold your head up high. It's gonna be all right, son," said Mama. "It's gonna be just fine."

I closed my eyes and went back to sleep.

I realize now what I couldn't comprehend then: we all may have a notion of how our story should go, but God is the ultimate storyteller. God takes us places that are unexpected and improbable. Once we get there, God places people in our lives who, if we are open to their words and deeds, will reshape our story. I believe God led me to University Hospital. I believe God's hand was on me during my stay. Things happened in that hospital that radically altered my thinking. In addition to renewing my relationship with my birth mother, I faced the issue of my homosexuality in ways that changed me forever. Because I had attempted suicide, I was admitted to that section of the hospital that dealt with mental disorders. A professional psychiatrist with impressive credentials was assigned to my case.

When I was first ushered into the office of Dr. Freund, I

didn't know what to expect. I was surprised and pleased when I saw a woman. It was easier for me to speak to women than to men. She spoke with a thick accent. She told me she had been educated in Europe and had come to Baltimore because of the fine reputation of Johns Hopkins and its sister hospitals like University. Dr. Freund was a small woman with large oval glasses. She rarely smiled—she was all business—but there was a kindness in her voice.

"Now tell me, Carl, what made you so unhappy that you swallowed all those pills?"

"My father. The way he talked to me. The way he hit me. He had never hit me before. I felt hate coming out of him. I had felt nothing but love from him before."

"And what caused all this?" she asked.

I didn't want to explain the situation to a stranger, especially a woman with a foreign accent who sat in an office with medical degrees on the wall. I didn't understand psychiatry. I thought that if I told her the truth, it would only get me into further trouble. She would side with my father, lock me up, and throw away the key. I didn't know what to think or say, so I said nothing.

"I understand why this is difficult for you," she said.

Did she?

How could she?

I still remained silent.

"Look, Carl," she said. "I want to help you. It's my job to help you. I don't want to harm you in any way. But in order to help you, I must understand what's troubling you. I'm not a policeman, Carl, and I'm not a judge. I can neither accuse nor condemn you of anything. You're free to speak your mind without fear of recrimination."

I had learned the word *recrimination* in school. I was proud of my vocabulary and proud to know that recrimination meant blame. Dr. Freund was saying that she wouldn't blame me for anything I had done. For reasons I can't explain, I was beginning to believe her. Yet I stayed silent.

"Carl," she continued, "let me begin by saying that many of the other young adults in here were also in desperate situations. Many of them decided that life was simply too painful. They preferred dying to living. This is an attitude which I can certainly understand."

"You can?"

"Of course I can. Especially when you are falsely accused of wrongdoing or, even worse, accused of doing something that is perfectly all right but seen as wrong. Does this make sense to you, Carl?"

It made perfect sense, but I still wasn't talking. I was listening.

"To understand you," the doctor went on, "I must know you. I must know not only what you are thinking but, more importantly, what you are feeling."

"I'm feeling afraid," I finally admitted.

"I understand," she said. "I'd be surprised if you weren't afraid. This is a new and scary experience for you. You have every right in the world to be afraid."

As Dr. Freund spoke, I felt less afraid. I felt myself willing— at least to some degree—to engage in conversation.

"When I tell you something," I asked, "will you tell my parents or my teachers?"

"Absolutely not," the doctor was quick to reply. "Our sessions are strictly confidential. I give you my word. I will never betray you, Carl."

"I felt like my parents have betrayed me," I finally said.

"How?"

"My father hit me and called me names. My mother let him do it. And none of it was my fault. All I did was tell the truth."

"About what?"

The only member of my family I'd told about my attraction to boys was my sister Martha, but something in Dr. Freund's spirit shattered my resistance. In a stream of words that must have gone on for fifteen minutes, I told her the full story about my uncle, my sexual experiences with boys, and this recent episode that had led me to swallow the pills. When I was through, I was still afraid that she might chide or punish me.

"Carl," she said, "I'm going to tell you something that I hope you'll remember for the rest of your life. Listen carefully. Many in my profession consider homosexuality a sickness. I do not. I am certain it is not. It is merely one of many sexual dispositions—sexual orientations—that characterize human beings. Some men are attracted only to men. Some only to women. And some to men *and* women. Women are similarly disposed. There are women who desire other women, others who desire men and women, and also women who are sexually drawn only to men. The reason we are made so differently remains a fundamental mystery that, I suspect, will never be completely understood. What matters most for you, though, is not to feel that anything is wrong with your sexuality. *There is nothing wrong.* You have no disease. You do not have to be cured. Am I being clear?"

I was startled. No statement had ever seemed clearer. But given my parents' attitude—given, for that matter, the secrecy with which homosexuality was practiced and the stigma surrounding it—how could the doctor be so certain that there was nothing "wrong" with it? In the black church community, no one discussed homosexuality. Yet many people didn't hide their gayness.

Right then I started thinking about Mom's first cousin Carroll, a gay gentleman who brought Andrew to our Thanksgiving table every year. Both men were government workers in D.C., well dressed and well spoken. They didn't hold hands or kiss in public, but they were clearly a couple. Dad didn't ban them and

Mom didn't chastise them. Sometimes, though, when Carroll and Andrew were in the kitchen helping with the dishes, I saw my aunts and uncles mimic their feminine mannerisms behind their backs. The mockery sent a message that even though Carroll and Andrew were welcome in our home, they were objects of ridicule.

In future sessions with Dr. Freund, I eventually told her the story of Cousin Carroll and Andrew.

"That's very interesting," she said, "and, I would imagine, very confusing for you, Carl. You watch your parents invite a cousin into your home. He and his friend are treated like a normal couple, but when they are made fun of, there is also another feeling conveyed to you—that something is very wrong with these men. They are seen as clowns. They are accepted but they are not accepted. It's hard for you to know what to think about them, or what to think about yourself. You obviously relate to them, but in doing so, you relate to men who are belittled. This is painful."

During my prolonged hospital stay, I looked forward to my weekly meetings with Dr. Freund. The more time I spent with her, the more questions I asked.

"If you think that homosexuality is okay," I said, "why does most everyone else feel differently?"

"That's a complicated question that I cannot answer simply, Carl. All I can say is that differences in sexuality have always been a problem for people. Sex is a powerful, powerful component. It drives us in so many ways. It defines us in so many ways. The world wants to think that there is only one kind of healthy sex—the kind between a man and a woman—because other varieties are confusing and, for many people, threatening. Many predominantly heterosexual men harbor homosexual feelings that they find uncomfortable. The same applies to heterosexual women who, from time to time, experience homosexual desire. Rather than live with such emotional complexities, people often prefer to deny them. As far as the psychiatric community goes—well, my profession has as many prejudices as any other.

"Think of it this way, Carl. As you have seen in your life, there are white people deeply prejudiced against Negroes. They don't want to accept you; they refuse to embrace your essential humanity. The same is true in the case of heterosexuals judging homosexuals. They also don't want to accept them or embrace their essential humanity. Our world isn't just. But from your perspective, the challenge is *not* to internalize the prejudiced judgment of the world."

"What does *internalize* mean, Dr. Freund?" I asked.

"Believe it, accept it, take it into your heart, and use it as a reason to belittle or dislike yourself."

In these discussions with Dr. Freund, I see the providential hand of God. The doctor and I did not mention religion. I don't even know if she was a believer. That hardly matters. What matters, though, is that a figure of great authority—a medical doctor trained in Europe with a specialty in psychiatry—validated who I was at the deepest level. Without her unequivocal affirmation, I would be a different person today. The bedrock of my security—the love from my adopted mother and father—had been taken from me. In this period, I required extraordinary support.

At that time, in the late fifties, during an era when homosexuality was called a sickness by doctors and a sin by clergymen, I was counseled by a physician who argued otherwise. Simultaneously, my blood mother accepted me without reservation. My presence in the hospital where she and her sister worked was miraculous. These beautiful women—my doctor, my mama, and my aunt Rosalie—nourished me with such deep love that instead of feeling cursed, I felt blessed.

On arrival, I had been put on suicide watch and given plastic utensils. I had no contact with other patients. But after several weeks, Dr. Freund moved me to another floor where I could interact with kids my age. This interaction proved profound.

My mornings began with recreational therapy in the hospital gym. City law required that we school-age patients be tutored to maintain our grade level. Three days a week, a teacher from the public schools came by and personally instructed me in all the mandatory subjects. This individualized educational attention was another blessing.

When Reverend Wood came to visit, he was loving and encouraging. Never once did he invoke Romans 1 or Leviticus 18:22, the passages regularly cited as condemnations of homosexuality in much the same way scripture was once used to justify slavery. Never once did my minister suggest I was going to hell or needed to change what the world saw as deviant behavior. He prayed for my peace of mind, for reconciliation between my parents and myself, and for all of us to find the wisdom to do God's will. His prayers brought me comfort. So did the head nurse.

"Carl," she said, "I go to Union Church and have a brother named John* who sings in the choir. Do you know him?"

I did know him. He was another gay boy in the gospel community.

"John's a great guy and a great brother," the nurse went on. "He reminds me of you. So just consider me your sister. And remember, Carl, no one here really thinks there's anything wrong with you. You have nothing to be ashamed of. I'm calling you baby bro, and I'm telling you that everyone loves you."

Everyone loves you! What a thing to hear in the psychiatric ward!

After a few weeks, Dr. Freund gave me permission to take an overnight leave. At first I was hesitant, but my godparents called the hospital and said that they wanted to see me. I left the hospital in a cheerful mood. I'm quick to forgive, and the fact that my father had struck me was softened by Dr. Freund's insistence that I'd done nothing wrong. She explained to me that my father's temper was his problem, not mine.

I was happy to be on the city streets again, and as I walked I boldly sang the songs of the day—"Charlie Brown" and "Yakety Yak." Passersby would nod and smile. I had a little pep in my step. But when I arrived home, the cheerfulness stopped. Dad was pleasant enough, but something had changed in Mom's attitude. Her resentment of me was more pronounced. At lunch, she served me in a tin pie plate while she and Dad ate on china. Instead of a regular glass, I was given a tin measuring cup. It was as if I were a second-class visitor and no longer their son. She didn't speak angry words to me, but there was anger in the way she ignored me.

A month later, I was allowed to leave the hospital again. This time I decided to go to Providence Baptist. I was excited to return to the church that had brought me so much joy. I put on the white robe of the gleaner and, along with the other youth, collected contributions. After the donations were made, I went to join my cohorts. This was always a time of chatter and goodwill. But as I approached my church friends, the chatter stopped. Dead silence. All eyes turned on me. No one smiled; no one said, "Welcome back, Carl." I felt a terrible chill and knew that my hospitalization, and the story that led to it, had turned my fellow gleaners against me. I was crushed. I left Providence that very day and never returned.

The hospital gave me a feeling of belonging denied by my church. There were patients from all walks of life, and I enjoyed interacting with many of them. The white kids in our ward had almost no personal contact with blacks and yet were friendly and curious about my background. Conversely, I was curious about theirs. Many had affluent parents who knew that University Hospital, a teaching hospital, had the best facilities in Baltimore.

Given the expense, only the well-to-do could afford this treatment. It was only because of Mama, an employee, that I didn't have to pay.

At first, we kids were uneasy around each other. After all, we were there because our behavior had reached an extreme point and, in many instances, a shameful one. But we soon realized that we needed friends to talk to who understood. We bonded. Inside that ward, society's walls dividing race, class, and religion tumbled down. Because the world had seen us as "kooks," because society had rejected us, our common link was strong. We were more than fellow patients. We were fellow sufferers, misunderstood by our families and culture. By speaking with these other kids—by listening to them with my heart as well as my ears—I transcended the small world in which I had been raised. I made close friends. Diana* was one.

Diana's dad was a lawyer, her mother a society lady whose picture often appeared in the paper for hosting a charity ball or attending the opening of the opera season. Diana was expected to follow in her mother's footsteps. There were plans to make her a debutante. But Diana rebelled. She couldn't have cared less about high society and hated the hypocrisy of that world. Instead she became a bohemian. She started drinking and smoking marijuana; she made a point to date the very boys her folks had prohibited her from seeing. Her current beau, for example, was Dale*, a juvenile delinquent straight out of the James Dean/ Elvis Presley mode—an angry young man in a black leather jacket, a Camel dangling from his lips. The very sight of Dale infuriated Diana's parents, which motivated Diana to see him even more. Sometimes after being with Dale all night, she came home drunk. Finally, her parents could take no more and had her committed to University Hospital. They decided that all this rebellion must mean that their daughter was mentally unstable.

To me, Diana was a supercool girl who was simply looking for love. Her parents, busy with their social life, gave her little attention and no affection. So she sought approval from other people in other ways. I saw her as a princess who had been cast out of her own home. She was an outsider like me.

Another white girl at University had been caught kissing her girlfriend. We didn't criticize or judge her. We understood. She was one of us.

A white boy came from a background similar to Diana's. His wealthy parents spent most of their time in Europe and left him alone to fend for himself. When they returned from their whirlwind trips and found their son was acting out—wrecking their car or drinking up all the liquor in the house—they couldn't understand why, so they decided to put him away.

The stories were fascinating to me. As we all dissected our lives, I realized the vastness of the world. When the other kids spoke about their private swimming lessons and ballet classes, I was amazed. All this was exotic but also moving—moving because, despite the riches, these kids were no better off than I was. In many cases, they were worse off. I had always received enormous amounts of love. They had not. I had always felt some sense of familial protection. They had not. They were strangers in their own homes.

The doctors allowed us to go on short-term leaves. For a couple of hours in the afternoon, we could leave the hospital and wander through downtown Baltimore. By then Diana and I were like brother and sister. She took great delight in scandalizing her parents, and I took even greater delight in hearing how she had done it—grabbing the keys to their Jaguar and going for joyrides; hosting crazy pool parties in the backyard when Mom and Dad were away; showing up at their exclusive country club on the back of Dale's motorcycle with Dale leathered up like Marlon Brando in *The Wild One*. It was Dale who met us right outside the hospital door on the day of our most memorable adventure.

As the three of us walked the bustling streets of downtown Baltimore, people gave us dirty looks. Dale looked like a hoodlum, Diana looked trampy, and what was a gay black boy doing with them anyway? We didn't care. The bigoted attitudes went right past us. If the world wanted to look down on us, that was the world's problem, not ours.

At Hecht's, the big department store, I gave Diana advice about how to put together a truly bohemian outfit. "Combine that quilted gypsy skirt with black leggings," I said, "and you'll have the year's sharpest look." Dale approved. At Woolworth's lunch counter, the waitress appraised us disapprovingly. Tough. We continued to laugh and joke. Behind the counter was a row of balloons and a sign for a special promotion for sundaes. We ordered three. Pop a balloon with a dart and a piece of paper would fall out with the price of your sundae—anywhere from a penny to thirty-nine cents. Diana's sundae was a dime. Dale's was a nickel. But when it was my turn to throw the dart, the waitress stopped me.

"He's not allowed to sit here," said the waitress. "It's against our policy."

That's all Diana and Dale needed to hear. They started shouting how it wasn't right, it wasn't legal, and we weren't going to move. They made me feel terrific. They protected me as no friends had ever protected me before. Diana and Dale caused such a fuss that a store supervisor came over and overruled the waitress. I was entitled to eat there. I was also entitled to throw my dart. When I threw it, and when my price was just a penny, we all screamed in victory. No sundae has ever tasted better.

Before leaving, Dale wanted to go over to the record department and check out the latest hits. He was crazy about Jerry Lee Lewis and Ray Charles. When we got there, the Drifters' "There Goes My Baby" was playing on a little phonograph for 45s. Diana and I did a little dance in the aisle while Dale searched the bins.

Back out on the street, the sun was shining. I felt just great—until a few seconds later when a man in a black suit shouted, *"Stop where you are!"* He said he worked for Woolworth's and knew we were carrying stolen merchandise. I didn't know what he was talking about, but Dale did. When he searched Dale, the detective discovered six or seven 45s he had lifted from the record department. I was shocked. But Diana seemed more excited than afraid.

"I know it's this guy's fault," said the detective, pointing to me. "I know you're both working for him."

"You're crazy," said Diana. "He had nothing to do with it."

"I don't believe you," the detective shot back. "It's the nigger who got you to steal."

"Like hell he did," said Dale. "He didn't even know what I was doing."

"Bullshit," said the detective. "But if that's how you want to play it, I'll haul all three of you down to jail."

Dale was indifferent. This wasn't his first time. Diana sensed a new adventure. I, of course, was petrified. I had never been to a police station in my life. They put us in a room where other detectives began accusing us. Outraged that I would be hanging out with white kids, they called me names and wanted all the details behind my "operation." When I told the simple truth—that I had not stolen a thing—I was mocked. When Diana and I said we were patients at University Hospital on a two-hour leave, no one believed us. Despite my urging, they wouldn't call the hospital. Finally, they called our parents.

Dale's parents never showed up. Diana's parents were out of town. But Harry and Jeter came down immediately. Mom was furious and, at first, Dad was too. But I could see that Dad's concern for my well-being quickly overwhelmed his anger. He understood that I had been falsely accused and saw that I needed both quick action and emotional support. The first thing he did was demand that the authorities call the hospital to confirm that Diana and I were patients. That's all it took. Once our status had been established, we were allowed to go.

"You can come home with us, Carl," said Dad.

"I can't do that, Dad," I said. I thanked him for his help, and then he and Mom walked out without me. I went back to the hospital with Diana. More than anywhere in the world, the hospital was the one place I felt safe.

The therapy continued, and so did the visits from my mother and Aunt Rosalie. The academic tutor came every other day and I kept up with my studies. I even had an occasional sexual encounter. One of the orderlies, a straight boy in his early twenties, came to my room after lights out. I didn't resist. I didn't want to resist. I wanted him and whatever love, affection, and physical pleasure he offered. Then, in one of our afternoon sessions, Dr. Freund told me that I would soon be released.

"You have made progress, Carl," she said. "You're no longer the confused and angry boy who showed up some ten months ago. When you were admitted, they told me that you were suicidal. They said you were having a nervous breakdown. But looking over this period of time, Carl, I can say that you've had a breakthrough instead. I think that you are now more accepting of yourself. I think you're ready to go home."

"I don't want to go to my mom and dad's home."

"I can understand that, but you have another mother, Carl— your natural mother, Arlene. Have you thought about going home with her?"

"Yes."

"Have you discussed it with her?"

"No."

"Will you?"

I said I would.

My mother was emptying out the wastebaskets in the ward when she spotted me doing math homework at a table by the window. She came over and kissed me on the cheek.

"Good morning, baby," she said. "I like it when you sit there studying your books. Makes me proud."

"Mama," I said, "Dr. Freund says I'll soon be released."

"That's wonderful, sugar. I know you're ready to get out of here. Harry and Jeter will be happy to have you back."

"I don't know if I want to go back to Harry and Jeter," I said.

The statement took Mama aback. Of course she knew the story of how my godfather had hit me—and the incident that led me here.

"I understand, baby," she said.

After a few seconds of silence, she uttered the words I was hoping to hear.

"You can come home with me, son. I don't have much, but whatever I have is yours."

I jumped up and hugged Mama with all my might.

BACK EAST

At the start of a new decade, with Jack Kennedy running for president and hope in the air, I was fifteen and back on the East Side, the neighborhood that Harry Smith had been so eager to leave. I was out of the clinic and in a drastically different environment than when I had entered University Hospital. Unlike my adoptive parents, Mama had never made financial progress in her life. She had had two more babies—Robin and Tony—by another man and lived in a row house in the middle of Chapel Street. The conditions were dirt poor. When I lived with Harry and Jeter, there was abundance—the refrigerator was well-stocked, my closet was crowded with clothes, and the house was filled with beautiful furniture. Mama had none of that. She barely made enough to feed herself and my little sister and brother. When she came home at night and I saw the sheer exhaustion on her face, I wanted to cry. She barely had the energy to make a meal or heat the formula. Mopping hospital floors for ten straight hours took a terrible toll. I wanted to do everything I could to help her. I had to help her because, in truth, she didn't have the money to feed me.

The first thing I said was, "Mama, I'll babysit the kids during the day. I'll take care of them." I loved my sister and brother—Tony was just a year old and Robin was three—and took pride in caring for them.

When it came to men, Mama really didn't take care of

herself. Her judgment wasn't good. She chose partners who were substance abusers and sometimes violent. When I came home from the hospital, one of her boyfriends often spent the night but contributed nothing to the household. He had no interest in finding a job, only in sex. He was also interested in me. Truth is, he probably had sex with me more often than he did with my mother. And he was not the only boyfriend of Mom's to do so.

I slept on the sofa, and every night after Norman went to the bathroom, he'd walk by me and expose himself. That kind of manipulation worked on me. Every morning, after Mama got up and went off to her job, I'd slip into her room, get under the covers, and give him oral sex. He kept his eyes closed and never—not once—acknowledged what was happening between us.

My tutoring program continued at home, which meant that I didn't have to return to school. My days were spent taking care of my siblings. I always helped Mama give them dinner and put them to sleep. When she fell asleep at the kitchen table or on the couch, it broke my heart to see how life was dragging her down.

Socially, I was going through a difficult period. The East Side boys and girls were telling me that I was not welcome in their homes. "Why?" I asked. "Because my daddy says you can't be around my little brothers. He says you're a sissy." I was looking for the comfort of another home and family. Instead, I was treated like a social outcast. During the summer, when other kids were on the stoops, playing, dancing, and listening to music, I sat by myself. In the midst of a bustling community, I was shamed and told I didn't belong. In those years, I certainly couldn't look in the white world for companionship. So when I was rejected by my own people, I was devastated.

I thank God for those neighborhood women who, like the angelic Miss Arlene, loved me unconditionally. When their husbands were at work, these ladies looked for me, wanting to know if I had eaten. They called me into their homes and gave me food, comfort, and prayer.

I ultimately found companionship with a group of gay boys who had no qualms about dressing up. Ever since I had discovered Jeter's black hat, I'd been intrigued by drag. Now to go out in drag was a new thrill. The other guys did so freely, as if it were the most natural thing in the world. We walked the streets in women's attire. We haunted certain hang-outs. We joked and danced and created an alternative universe in which we reinvented ourselves as carefree young women in love with life.

We were mentored and mothered by a group of older queens who had been dragging for years. Some of them were also boosters, thieves who specialized in stealing fashionable clothing from department stores. Consequently we had access to many beautiful things, and the older queens let us wear what we liked. I was an avid reader of *Vogue*, and my taste leaned toward tailored slacks and well-cut silk blouses. One of the more experienced queens taught me how to wear my hair in a French twist with perfectly cut bangs. Many of those queens—both my age and older—remained lifelong friends and are still in my life today.

I also had a large group of female friends who consulted me for fashion advice. We scoured *Seventeen* magazine and shopped together in Baltimore's best stores. I'd sit outside the dressing room and tell them which outfits suited them best.

I also snuck in to the Royal Theatre, Baltimore's answer to the Howard in Washington, the Regal in Chicago, and the Apollo in New York. When I was a kid, Dad had taken me to the Royal for live shows *and* movies. I saw *The Robe* followed by Faye Adams singing "Shake a Hand" and the Dominoes doing "Have Mercy, Baby." As a teenager, I went to the Royal alone. I bought a front-row ticket and, with the rest of the audience, screamed when the Coasters sang "Yakety Yak," "Charlie Brown," and "Poison Ivy." I screamed loudest when Cornell Gunther did his dead-on impression of Miss Dinah Washington's "What a Difference a Day Makes." Miss Cornell sounded more like Miss Dinah than Miss Dinah herself. To all the queens in the crowd, his feminine mannerisms made it clear that he was one of us. That was also true of Rudy Lewis of the Drifters, whose voice gave chills to teen audiences. The gay presence in our cultural dynamic was always there. The Jewel Box Revue, a sensational drag show, played the Apollo to standing-room-only crowds for many years. Later, Lester Wilson, in his choreography for the TV show *Solid Gold,* and Michael Peters, in his choreography for Michael Jackson, would assert a spirited gay aesthetic.

Something else occurred during this period of my life that is not easy for me to disclose. I've suppressed the memory and never revealed it to a single soul. The simple truth is that during this period when I was desperate to contribute to Mama's household, I sold sexual favors. At first when I arrived in the neighborhood and saw certain older men wink at me, I ignored them. I turned down what were obvious solicitations. But the longer I lived with Mama, the more I saw her desperate situation, the more I felt compelled to help her. In the world of greater Baltimore, no one was about to hire an underage openly effeminate boy like me. No part-time jobs were available. Moreover, I was still in my post-hospitalization state of confusion and uncertainty.

The acts themselves were repulsive. I closed my eyes and pretended to be elsewhere. But I did them nonetheless. There was an older man who came through the neighborhood with a horse-drawn wagon. In exchange for sex, he gave me a week's worth of vegetables and potatoes. There was a man who sold fish, a storefront preacher, a grocery store owner, and a white policeman, all of whom paid for sex. With some of the other queens, I would occasionally work Baltimore Street, the red-light district only three blocks from City Hall where businessmen and sailors looked for prostitutes of all kinds. I sold myself both in and out of drag. It didn't matter. I simply needed money.

In order to give the money to Mama, I had to lie. "Grandma gave me this ten dollars," I'd say, or Aunt Donna or Aunt Sue. Mama could never know the truth.

Then something happened that changed everything: Mama became pregnant.

Mama hoped that once Norman learned she was expecting, he'd find a job and contribute to our household. He didn't. Instead, he disappeared. Part of me wanted to tell Mama about Norman and me, but I didn't have the heart. The revelation would have only hurt her.

The pregnancy proved difficult. I did my best to help out with the babies and take pressure off Mama. Her energy was low and her spirit sinking fast. One evening, while I was feeding my sister and brother, Mama called me up to her room. She was in bed, her body trembling. "When a woman comes to the door," she said, her voice barely audible, "please let her in."

The woman was a nurse from the hospital. She stayed in my mother's room an hour or so. Then she left in a great hurry, without a word to me. Minutes later, I heard my mother moaning. I ran upstairs. There was blood everywhere. Mama could hardly breathe; in a whispery voice, she asked me to blow into her mouth. When that didn't seem to do any good, she asked me to rub her chest, thinking that would help her breathe. I rubbed so hard that her skin came up under my fingers. Now her voice was gone, but her eyes said, *Help!* That look between us was our last communication and haunts me to this day.

I ran around the corner to fetch my grandmother, my dad's mom. From what I told her, she knew it was a botched abortion and, fearing the law, wanted no part of it.

"She'll be all right," said Grandma. "Let her be."

I ran back home. Mama was in agony. She was hemorrhaging

blood. I sped back to Grandma's, shouting, *"You gotta get Mama to the hospital! You gotta do it right now!"* Finally Grandma, along with Aunt Rosalie and two of my uncles, sprang into action. Afraid of the authorities, they didn't call an ambulance but brought Mama to the hospital themselves. As they dragged her into their car, her head hit the concrete front steps. Finally they got her in and rushed off to the hospital.

The next twenty-four hours were horrible. I was alone with the babies, who were crying their eyes out. I was afraid Norman would show up and want sex. I called the hospital to see about Mama's condition but never got through. Finally, early the next morning, I heard a knock on the door. Two white women were standing there.

"Is this the home of Arlene?" the first one asked.

"Yes."

"Who are you?"

"Carl, her son."

"Well, your mother is dead."

Having delivered the news, they turned and left. My heart felt like it would explode. I grew dizzy and faint. I was sick to my stomach. It was the worst moment of my life. What would become of the babies? What would become of me? And what if Norman came back? The world had become cold-blooded, indifferent, and frightening. I had had only one year with my birth mother, and she was gone.

Harry and Jeter Smith, who both had lost their mothers, could not have been kinder. They came to claim me.

"You'll come back home," they said. "We'll see to it that those babies are given proper care."

The week of the funeral, I returned to the home I had left when I had been committed to University Hospital. Mom and Dad did everything they could to heal my broken heart. The nightmare of Mama's deadly abortion, though, was not over. The state prosecuted the nurse who had run out of the house and left Mama to die. Only one person could identify her—me. I was called down to the courthouse to testify. I put on a coat and tie and went downtown with members of Mama's family. I never expected to be facing the family of the accused nurse. They were all there in the courtroom, looking at me with murder in their eyes.

Before the trial began, I went to the men's room. Two of the nurse's male relatives followed. While I was washing my hands, they threatened me with their fists. I started screaming, "Help!"

Before I knew it, my uncles ran in and rescued me. By then it was time for my testimony.

"Is that the woman?" the judge asked me.

As I looked at her, she turned away.

"Yes," I told the judge.

The woman lost her nurse's license.

I went back to my adopted parents' house on Lauretta Avenue. My soul stayed sick for a long time. It wasn't that I harbored animosity toward Harry and Jeter. The pill incident was long behind us. But I was still uneasy in their home. Even more, I was never comfortable in Baltimore again.

For years, I had been reading about New York City and, in particular, Greenwich Village. I learned that many homosexuals lived there, that gay men could openly congregate in coffeehouses and bars. I dreamt about the artistic ambience of that neighborhood where everyone was a dancer, poet, musician, or painter. When I was in the Jackie Robinson Youth Council, I had learned about Harlem and the Harlem Renaissance. Our leaders talked about Duke Ellington, who lived on Sugar Hill, and black writers who expressed the soul of our people. Teachers in Baltimore's civil rights movement had told us about the novelist James Baldwin and the composer Billy Strayhorn, gay men celebrated for their beautiful talent. We had seen pictures of the

Apollo Theater, where Ella Fitzgerald had won an amateur contest, and Minton's Playhouse, where Dizzy Gillespie and Charlie Parker had invented modern jazz. I knew that Adam Clayton Powell Jr. preached in the Abyssinian Baptist Church and that Sugar Ray Robinson ran a restaurant where all the fabulous people rubbed shoulders.

New York City was where I wanted to be. I wanted to leave my past behind—all the hurt, the pain, the unfulfilled dreams. In my imagination, my dreams would come true in New York.

After I moved back to the West Side, the tutor from University Hospital schooled me at home. That was fine. But I also knew that once I turned sixteen, state law allowed me to do as I pleased. I could give up the tutor and quit school entirely. The choice between high school and New York City was an easy one. In May 1960, days after turning sixteen, I told my foster parents that I was leaving. They didn't try to stop me. They knew I'd been through hell.

Dad drove me to the Greyhound station and handed me a wad of money. We both had tears in our eyes. "You're gonna make it, son," he said. "I know something about this mean ol' world, and I know you got what it takes." He hugged me tight. Then I boarded the bus for New York.

THE CITY

You can't imagine the excitement I felt when I stepped off that bus at the Port Authority Terminal on Forty-second Street. Like Dorothy entering Oz, my world went from black-and-white to Technicolor. Out with the throngs on Eighth Avenue, I felt like Doris Day in a Rock Hudson movie. I was in love with Manhattan, the crowds of people, the electric energy, the bold skyscrapers, the honking yellow taxis, in love with life in the great metropolis.

I walked down to the Sloane House Y on Thirty-fourth Street, where the rooms where cheap. That first night I went out walking. After a gentle rain, the air was fresh. I strolled up Broadway to Times Square to see the gaudy lights, then over to Fifth Avenue to window-shop at the fancy department stores, then up Park Avenue, where white-gloved doormen helped women in evening gowns into gleaming black limousines. Back at the Y, I was up all night, too excited to sleep. My great adventure had begun.

Naturally, I needed a job. I got the morning paper, scanned the want ads, and saw that Macy's was looking for stock boys. According to a banner out front, Macy's was the biggest store in the world. It dominated Herald Square, the small park where Broadway converged with Sixth Avenue at Thirty-fourth Street. I walked through the mammoth store to the personnel department.

"Can you read?" the lady asked me.

"Of course I can read. I read well."

"Can you write?"

"Yes, ma'am. I write well."

"You'll have to take a test."

"I'll be glad to."

I passed with flying colors and the job was mine. Minimum wage was barely a dollar an hour, but any wage sounded good to me. The underground world at Macy's was as fascinating as—maybe even more fascinating than—its vast retail sections. The sprawling basement was a maze of hallways where carts loaded with merchandise rolled up and down the length and breadth of the store. This hidden world of workers, mainly Puerto Ricans and African Americans, was exotic. There was high-pitched chatter and gaiety. There were men and women of all ages, all skin tones, all temperaments. I was put in the gift-wrap department with mainly older ladies, who taught me the tricks of the trade. I caught on quickly and soon became an ace wrapper.

The underground culture at Macy's, like all cultures, was multidimensional. Among the young people, straight guys were cruising the gals. There was also a contingent of gay guys. One day during our lunch break I was singing a gospel song when a black guy, who had come to the city from South Carolina, approached me.

"Oh, my Lord," he said. "You sound like you need to go to Christian Tabernacle."

Even back in Baltimore, I had heard of that church.

"Isn't it up in Harlem?" I asked.

"Yes, baby," the guy said. "It is *the* church in Harlem. You been to Harlem yet?"

"No," I admitted.

"Well, honey, if you haven't been to Harlem, you haven't been to New York."

"I want to go."

"You *got* to go."

"How do you get there?"

"How you think you get there?"

"I don't know."

"You take the A train, baby. Haven't you heard the song? The A train's 'the quickest way to get to Harlem.'"

That Sunday, I took the A train, got off at 125th Street, and walked past the Apollo Theater, where the marquee announced the Drifters, the Miracles, the Marvelettes, and Bobby "Blue" Bland. I walked past the clothing stores, the jewelry stores, the wig stores, the restaurants, and the bars. And right there, on the same 125th Street, only three blocks down from the Apollo, above a store that sold baby clothes, was the Christian Tabernacle Church.

The minute I entered, I knew I was home. You didn't have to tell me that this was a predominantly gay church. I saw it, felt it, and loved it. And I loved Reverend William Morris O'Neill, who had come from Chicago, where he had studied with Clarence H. Cobbs at the First Church of Deliverance. Chicago was the center of our modern church music, the home of Mahalia Jackson, the Queen of Gospel, and Thomas Andrew Dorsey, the Father of Gospel.

The charismatic Reverend Cobbs, widely known to be gay, was considered the most popular black preacher in America. He lived in a mansion next to Elijah Muhammad and vacationed with Mahalia Jackson. The First Church of Deliverance had the first black choir to enjoy a national audience on network radio. It was at Cobbs's church that the Hammond B-3 organ became a staple of the African American gospel sound. Back in the forties, one of Cobbs's musicians, Kenneth Morris, worked for Hammond as a demonstrator. After he brought an organ into the First Church of Deliverance, gospel music was never the same.

I had never heard a preacher like Cobbs's protégé, Reverend

O'Neill. O'Neill was clearly bi, extremely loving, and brilliant in the pulpit. Suddenly, then, I found myself in the center of the Golden Age of Gospel at a time when the giants still walked the earth; the great gospel singers were alive, well, and, with their thundering Holy Ghost spirit, still wrecking churches from coast to coast.

They all came to Christian Tabernacle—Mahalia (who was "Haley" to us), Marion Williams, Albertina Walker and the Caravans, Clara Ward and the Famous Ward Singers, and the incomparable Professor Alex Bradford, another flashy gospel superstar known as "the Singing Rage of the Gospel Age." They came to Christian Tabernacle because Reverend O'Neill presided over the baddest gospel sounds this side of Chicago.

The first time I attended the Sunday evening service, I was amazed by the people: everyone dressed in white. The women wore white dresses, white gloves, white stockings, and white shoes; the men wore white trousers, white shirts, and white shoes. Reverend Cobbs had initiated the tradition in Chicago during the Great Depression to free his congregation of elitism and class divisions. He didn't want the well-to-do members showing off their clothes. He wanted everyone to feel equal in the eyes of God. O'Neill carried on this tradition in Harlem.

The fact that Christian Tabernacle was just down the street from the Apollo had more than geographic significance. When Thomas A. Dorsey, writer of, among many other songs, "Take My Hand, Precious Lord," brought blues and jazz voicings into gospel, the nature of our music changed. The gap between secular and sacred narrowed, and eventually genres overlapped. In the fifties, when Ray Charles used gospel motifs to write songs like "I Got a Woman" and "Yes Indeed," rhythm and blues became gospel-filled. Sam Cooke, the biggest gospel star in the country, became the biggest R & B star. Later in the sixties, Aretha Franklin would intensify the merger between church and state with remarkable results.

I could feel the closeness of these two forms in this Harlem church. Once I joined the choir and attended every Sunday service, I would see R & B stars at our church. I'd look out from the choir and see Jackie Wilson or Dinah Washington, Ruth Brown or Etta James in the congregation.

As a singer, I had one of the voices that carried over the entire Christian Tabernacle Choir. It wasn't anything I tried to do. By nature, I'm a belter, and a belter, even in a big choir, gets heard. Some fellow singers approached me.

James was from South Carolina, Wilbur, another belter, from North Carolina, and Bart from New York.

"Hey, Carl," said Wilbur, "we're starting a group and want you to join."

I was flattered.

"What will we call ourselves?" asked James.

"We got soul," said Wilbur, "and we're singing gospel, so we're the Gospel Souls."

Of the four members, I was the least experienced and knew the fewest songs. But that didn't keep my brothers from demanding that I sing lead. Around this time, the great Shirley Caesar, a Caravan, had a hit song, "No Coward Soldier," an assertive gospel number that required a ferocious lead. I was tapped to sing Shirley's part, but when we started rehearsing, I was hesitant. Providence Baptist in Baltimore had had far calmer music, anthems like, "How Lovely Are Thy Dwellings." This kind of gut-busting, tell-it-on-the-mountain groove was new for me.

"Just sing!" the guys urged. "Just go on and sing!"

After we had rehearsed for a week or so, Reverend O'Neill made an announcement from the pulpit.

"We're blessed to introduce a new group formed by our very own choir. They call themselves the Gospel Souls, and rumor has it that these boys can actually sing."

Standing in front of the packed church, I wasn't sure what would happen. After all, this was my debut. My legs were shaking and my mouth was dry. When I opened my mouth, though, sounds came out. God came out. God was sure enough watching over me that morning, because the sounds were strong. The response from the congregation was immediate and beautiful.

"Sing your song, boy!"

"Go on now!"

"My, my, my!"

"Praise him! Go on and praise him!"

There's nothing like singing in front of a group of believers eager to give you support and show you love. The Gospel Souls gained a local reputation, and soon we were performing during afternoon gospel programs in Brooklyn and the Bronx.

I met another wonderful singer in the choir who became my friend for life, the great Estelle Brown. One day after choir rehearsal, Estelle showed me a photograph of a woman. Looking at it, she began to cry.

"Who is that?" I asked.

"My blood mother," said Estelle. "She passed on."

I took out a picture of Arlene.

"This is my blood mother," I said. "She's also gone. I was raised by a foster mom."

"Me too," Estelle replied.

And with that, our bond was formed. Estelle took me to Brooklyn, where I met her foster mom, Miss Hannah, a Pentecostal Christian of towering faith and iron-clad strictness. Miss Hannah had raised a bunch of foster kids, including Estelle's blood siblings. They and Estelle had formed a group: brother Edward played piano and sang; Estelle sang lead; Jenette, who wound up with the Ruth Davis Singers, sang the top part; and Judy Wilcox sang harmony. They called themselves the Twilight Gems. In embracing me, they brought me deeper into the world of ambitious young church singers honing their craft in New York City.

I spent long hours singing and laughing with Estelle and Judy. I loved being one of the girls. Judy and I were walking through Harlem one afternoon with nothing to do, just two crazy kids looking to get into some harmless mischief.

"Let's sneak into this bar," said Judy. "I know the bartender."

She pointed to the Fantasia, just a block from the Apollo. It was a classy bar, with mirrored walls and upscale décor, that catered to gay men. The flashy jukebox immediately caught my eye. I slipped in a dime and pressed the button for Martha and the Vandellas. When "Dancing in the Street" came blasting out, I sang lead over Miss Martha. After I was through, I noticed that Judy was speaking to an especially effeminate gentleman. She motioned me over to his table. Later I learned that the gentleman had asked Judy, "Who's that boy singing at the jukebox?"

"That's Carl from Baltimore," Judy had answered.

"Well, tell Carl from Baltimore to come over here."

The gentleman asked me, "Where did you learn to sing like that, boy?"

"I don't really know," I answered.

"Well, I like your voice," he said. "What's your name?"

"Carl Bean."

"I'm Alex Bradford."

Alex Bradford! Professor Alex Bradford's song "Too Close to Heaven" was one of the biggest hits in gospel history. He had been Mahalia Jackson's personal secretary, written songs for Roberta Martin, and recorded a wildly popular duet with Sallie Martin, "He'll Wash You Whiter than Snow." Bradford had been minister of music at Newark's Greater Abyssinian Baptist on Lyons Avenue, where jazz producer John Hammond had recorded a live Bradford performance for Columbia Records, *Shakin' the Rafters*, a seminal album that crossed over to the nongospel market. He was known for his flamboyance as well as his artistry. Some called him the Little Richard of gospel.

"I'm staying at the Cecil Hotel," said Bradford. "I'll get you a room over there and tomorrow you can take the train and meet me in Newark. That way I can give you a real audition with my group."

I thought he was joking. I looked at Judy, who read my mind.

"Professor Bradford's not kidding, are you, professor?" she asked.

"I'm serious as serious can be," he said.

That night Judy and I slept at the Cecil, the famous Harlem hotel where the stars stayed. Downstairs was Minton's, the club that gave birth to bebop. Next morning, Judy and I went to Bradford's home in Newark. It was an amazing place, red silk drapes covering the windows, a mink spread covering the bed. Alex explained the situation: his group was going to London to appear in the off-Broadway musical *Black Nativity* by Langston Hughes. Langston had called it a "gospel song play" and rendered it, as only he could, as a reinvention of Saint Luke's biblical narrative using poetry, song, and dance. The show had been a big hit in New York. In Newark, Alex asked me to sing various parts—lead, background, baritone, tenor—and when he saw that I could handle them all, he said, "Carl Bean, how'd you'd like to go to England?"

My heart jumped for joy. "Yes, sir!" I said. "I'd love to go to England."

"No, Carl, you're not going to England."

"But Mom," I said on the phone, "this is the chance of a lifetime. This is Alex Bradford. This is a musical, a Christian musical, with beautiful costumes. We'll be performing on a big stage in London."

But she was adamant. Because I wasn't twenty-one, I needed my godmother's permission.

"Sorry, son, but London's too far. Bad enough you're up there in New York where your father and I can't keep our eye on you. But we are not signing a piece of paper that says you can fly across the ocean and start living in London."

"I won't be living there permanently."

"You won't be living there at all. And that's that, Carl."

When I told Alex I couldn't get my parents' consent, he was disappointed and started looking for another singer. I was crushed. I was back with the Gospel Souls, playing little concerts in church basements. After one of those concerts, fortune smiled again. A man named Calvin White approached me. Calvin had once sung second lead with Alex Bradford.

"I like your sound," he said.

"Why, thank you."

"I got my own group," he added. "The Gospel Wonders. Ever hear of us?"

I had. The Gospel Wonders were well known in New York.

"You ever sing professionally?" asked Calvin.

"Almost," I said.

"What does 'almost' mean?"

"I almost went with Alex Bradford to London, but my mom wouldn't allow it."

"Do you realize you were auditioning to take my place?"

"Wow! What a coincidence!"

"Well, we're not going to London, but we have lots of work around New York City. You interested?"

"I am."

"Great. Come round for an audition. We rehearse at Rainbow Studios on Forty-third and Eighth Avenue."

It was an all-male group, and I fit into their blend just fine. When he heard me sing, Calvin said, "Miss Bradford won't be getting this one. This one is mine!"

Just like that, I went from being an unpaid Gospel Soul to a paid Gospel Wonder. We had enough gigs so I could leave my job at Macy's and, even better, leave the Sloane House Y. Calvin said I could stay with him at his apartment on Henry Street in Greenwich Village.

Naturally I was thrilled. I'd walked through the Village many times, dreaming that maybe one day I could live there. I loved the quaint little streets, the antique shops, bookstores, and corner cafés. I also loved how openly gay people could be seen everywhere. Estelle Brown often came down to visit. Calvin knew her from when, as a kid, she had been with the Twilight Gems, a youth group known to sing as hard as adults. He asked her to join the Wonders.

"I just wrote this song," he said, "and I can hear Estelle singing lead."

Calvin started singing the song to me—"As long As I've Got Jesus."

"What do you think?" he asked.

The tune was catchy, the lyrics were original, and the rhythm right. "It's a smash," I said.

"I've talked to Herman Lubinsky over at Savoy about letting us record it," said Calvin. "We'll be going over to his studio in Newark next week."

The modern jazz geniuses—Charlie Parker, Miles Davis, Fats Navarro, Dexter Gordon, among a wealth of others—had made breakthrough recordings at Savoy, whose roster also included vocalist Little Jimmy Scott and R & B stars Johnny Otis and Little Esther Phillips. In gospel, Savoy had enjoyed megahits with the Gay Sisters, the Davis Sisters, the Roberta Martin Singers, the Ward Singers, Alex Bradford, Marion Williams, the Gospel Harmonettes, and the Caravans. At the start of the sixties, Savoy's owner Lubinsky had signed James Cleveland, who became his biggest moneymaker. The label's main gospel producers were Fred Mendelsohn and Reverend Lawrence Roberts, who specialized in choirs.

My first recording session! I couldn't wait. Our prerecording rehearsal was intense. The group met in Harlem on a Saturday before our Monday morning session in Newark. We were all excited when the great English soul singer, Dusty Springfield, showed up at rehearsal accompanied by Madeline Bell, who had been a Bradford Singer, along with Calvin White, during the *Black Nativity* run in London. That's where Dusty, Madeline, and Calvin had become friends. Madeline wanted to show Dusty Harlem.

We were Dusty fans, and we wanted her to sing along with us.

"Oh, no," she said at first. "I can't sing gospel."

"Girl," I said, "you can sing anything."

Reluctantly, Dusty started singing, and the result was magical. She blended in beautifully. That evening, when we walked over to a rib restaurant on 125th Street, singing all the way, she came along, absolutely thrilled to be in the heart of Harlem. Rapport was easy and natural. Her heart was with black people and black music. For those many hours we were together, Dusty became a Gospel Wonder!

On Monday, we made the short drive over to Newark. Savoy was located at 58 Market Street in the Ironbound district. The recording studio was upstairs. Downstairs was a record shop where you could also buy electronic parts for phonographs and tape recorders.

Lubinsky had a reputation for never paying royalties. In a hard-nosed business, he was the toughest of the tough. I didn't have business on my mind. I was just glad to be standing in front of a microphone where Clara Ward and Big Maybelle had once stood. We cut the record in no time. Estelle sang a magnificent lead, and I sang backup. The lyrics—"I've been lied on, cheated, talked about, and mistreated"—were dynamite. The groove was infectious.

When we sang it live in New York, folks stomped and hollered until we sang it again. Right off the bat, our record became a turntable hit in Harlem. The Gospel Wonders were on the map. We opened a program one Sunday at Christian Tabernacle. Reverend O'Neill loved us. The crowd went berserk, and none of the other acts wanted to follow us. James Cleveland happened to be there. In addition to being a musical genius, he was also a crafty businessman. The next day he went over to Newark and spoke to Lubinsky about this new hit, "As Long as I've Got Jesus." He wanted to record it. Well, Calvin White had written it, but he had given his publishing rights to Lubinsky. That meant Lubinsky controlled it. And although our version of the song was being played on New York gospel radio, Lubinsky knew that a James Cleveland version would soar nationally.

Lubinksy was right. James's record buried ours. It became one of his biggest hits, and people thought he'd written it. The Gospel Wonders, meanwhile, had been embraced by the city's biggest gospel deejay, Joe Bostic, who started calling us "Harlem's own." We became New York's first-call gospel group. Backed by a Rockefeller Foundation grant to support the arts in Harlem, we performed on flatbed trucks along with Count Basie, vocalist Gloria Lynne—who had a big hit with "I Wish You Love"—and jazz avant-gardist Sun Ra. Whether at Mount Morris Park on 122nd Street or in the band shell at Central Park, audiences from all five boroughs fell in love with us.

Meanwhile, I was falling in love. It was a torrid, head-over-heels love that had me reeling and marked the end of one phase of my life and the start of another.

BABY BOY

As Marvin Gaye so eloquently expressed in "Heard It Through the Grapevine," "it took me by surprise, I must say." For me, "it" was a man. I'll call him Lawrence.

I was living with Calvin on Henry Street in the Village. He was making robes for the Gospel Wonders. He could do it all—create the designs, make the patterns, select fabrics, do the fittings, and sew the garments. I was standing on a stool in the living room while Calvin was taking my measurements for a new outfit when suddenly the door opened. In walked Lawrence, a friend of Calvin's.

I had never seen a man that gorgeous. He had a smoldering dark complexion, burning brown eyes, and a beautiful figure. Like Calvin, Lawrence was some seven years older than me. He lived in Philadelphia but often came to New York to visit Calvin. Sometimes he came with Jackie Verdell, a mighty gospel artist also living in Philly. Calvin and Jackie had become friends when she was with the Davis Sisters, whose early hits—"We Need Power" and "Lord, Don't Leave Me"—I had memorized.

Jackie's voice was a force of nature; she sang with tremendous power, passion, and originality. She and Clara Ward were Aretha Franklin's primary influences. Like Clara, Jackie was extremely close to Aretha's dad, the preacher whom gospel folk called Frank—Reverend C. L. Franklin of Detroit's New Bethel Baptist Church.

The four of us—Jackie, Lawrence, Calvin, and me—formed a tight social circle. Jackie and I adored each other; she became my older sister and I became her confidante. Meanwhile, Lawrence, who called me Baby Boy, became my lover. Spending the night at Calvin's, he slipped into my room and into my dreams. Nothing could keep me from surrendering to this beautiful man. It felt like the first truly grown-up love affair of my life. Lawrence's trips to New York became more frequent. When he went back to his business job in Philly, we talked by phone every day. The minute he showed up in New York, we were back in each other's arms. Sometimes I traveled to Philly to see both him and Jackie.

"I'm singing pop now," Jackie told me. "I got this deal with Decca."

Unfortunately, she never had a secular hit. Her records like "I'm Your Girl" and "Are You Ready for This?" fell short of the charts. Some argued that her voice was too gospel to be accepted by mainstream audiences. At the time—the early sixties—Aretha was having problems at Columbia Records. Her records weren't selling. But in 1967 she moved to Atlantic. When she recorded "I Never Loved a Man" and "Respect," produced by Jerry Wexler, she rediscovered her churchy soul. Like Ray Charles, Aretha married gospel to pop. Well, why couldn't a singer of Jackie's magnitude, who had inspired Aretha to sing, also enjoy that kind of success?

"Baby Boy," Jackie would tell me, "there's more to this music business than just talent. There's more than just timing, or luck, or influential contacts. There's a mystery that ain't ever gonna be solved—why some folk make it big, and some don't."

Jackie was great company, not only because of her upbeat spirit, but because she introduced me to jazz singers like Little

Jimmy Scott and Morgana King. She would also talk to me about the music biz. She taught me about stage presence.

"Baby Boy," she once said, "you have a voice like Brother Joe May."

"That's a big compliment, Jackie."

"You bet it is. They call Joe the Thunderbolt of the Middle West, but you could be the Cyclone of the East. You're capable of destroying any church you sing in. You can take it as far as you wanna."

"I like singing with the Wonders," I said.

"The Wonders are cool," Jackie agreed. "But you gotta get past the Wonders. You got a big voice like Solomon Burke. You've got a soulful voice like Ray Charles. If you want to sing rhythm and blues, Baby Boy, you can sing rhythm and blues."

I did want to sing rhythm and blues. But even beyond that, I wanted to sing everything. I wanted to sing Broadway. I wanted to be Ethel Merman in *Gypsy* and Barbra Streisand in *Funny Girl*; I wanted to be David Ruffin of the Temptations singing "My Girl." Meanwhile, though, I was happy to be a Gospel Wonder. With deejay Joe Bostic's help, we were gigging. I could call myself a pro.

Whenever the Wonders sang, Lawrence was right there in the first row, shouting "Sing, Baby Boy, sing!" My other major supporters were Cissy Houston and Judy Clay, who had been with the Drinkard Singers, Cissy's family group. (Judy was also the female half of the first recorded interracial vocal duo, with Billy Vera, who hit with "Storybook Children.") Cissy is Whitney's mom; Cissy's sister Lee, also a Drinkard singer, is the mother of Dee Dee and Dionne Warwick. Like Alex Bradford, the Drinkards, whom Mahalia Jackson had sponsored, were based in Newark, that bastion of gospel greatness. Cissy's family came out of New Hope Baptist.

My love for Lawrence, which I thought would last forever,

lasted six months. My cruel awakening happened on a Sunday afternoon. Lawrence had come to church to hear me sing, but when the service was over, he was nowhere to be found. Not understanding why he had slipped off without me, I drowned my sorrow in a postchurch lunch with a few choir members. We were sitting in a restaurant on Lenox Avenue when I looked up from my omelet to see Lawrence getting into a cab with a young man my age. I couldn't believe it. I dropped my fork and ran out of the restaurant, crying Lawrence's name. But by the time I got outside, the cab was in motion. I should have let it go. I should have gone back inside and finished my eggs. But fool that I was, I started chasing the cab down Lenox Avenue, crying, "Lawrence, come back! Lawrence, don't do this! Lawrence, I love you!"

I was a little pathetic, but young love—*naïve* young love—always is. It turned out that Lawrence was a player who had worked his way through a number of gospel choirs, plucking out the ripest fruits. I was devastated and cried for days.

It took a while, but my heart healed, thanks to the exciting world in which I found myself—the young people's gospel world of New York. I met wonderful people like Nick Ashford and Valerie Simpson, who were making the leap from sacred to secular. Through Estelle Brown, I also became friendly with the singers who simply referred to themselves as the Girls. They were church singers with a beautiful blend. Besides Estelle, the Girls were Sylvia Shemwell, Myrna Smith, and my friend and fan Cissy Houston. They infused everything with a full-bodied gospel flavor.

One day Estelle told me, "Cissy's got a session over at the Brill Building. Why don't you come along?"

I was ready to rock and roll. The Brill Building, on Broadway just above Times Square, was famous as the headquarters of music publishers with their roster of soon-to-be-legendary pop songwriters. When Estelle and I walked into the ornate lobby, I expected the upstairs offices to look the same. But instead there were endless rows of tiny cubicles barely big enough to hold a piano and a bench. Walking down the hall, I could hear doo-wop and girl groups grinding out three-part harmonies.

"This is Baby Boy," said Estelle, introducing me to Dionne, Dee Dee, and the others. I watched them do background work for some of the most famous producers and artists of the day. There were Jerry Leiber and Mike Stoller, who had written and produced the Coasters and were working with the Dixie Cups on "Chapel of Love" and "Iko Iko." Jeff Barry, Ellie Greenwich, and Shadow Morton were working with the Shangri-Las on "Leader of the Pack" and "Remember (Walkin' in the Sand)." Up and down the corridors, I saw Neil Diamond, Phil Spector, Carole King, and Bobby Darin. Someone said, "There's Florence Greenberg, the woman behind the Shirelles." Someone else said, "There's Jerry Wexler, a big shot at Atlantic Records, the label of Ruth Brown and Ray Charles."

I couldn't get enough of the Brill Building. If a male voice was needed, I was often recruited. I could sing baritone and tenor. I could also sing falsetto and seamlessly harmonize with the Girls. I learned the ins and outs of studio work—use of head-phones, mic technique, overdubbing. Meanwhile, in addition to her duties doing background, Dionne Warwick had been working as a demo singer for Burt Bacharach and Hal David, who were also part of the Brill Building crowd. Burt knew how to utilize Dionne's unusual and lilting vocal sensibility, and soon, rather than simply turning out demos, she was recording Bacharach/David compositions. "Don't Make Me Over" was her first hit, with her sister Dee Dee, Sylvia Shemwell, and Cissy doing the backgrounds. From then on, Dionne was off to the races.

Burt took a professional interest in me. He agreed to hear me sing at his fabulous apartment on Sutton Place. I felt like I was on a 1940s movie set. There were gorgeous silk curtains and plush couches, beautiful photographs of Burt's dog running along the beach, and a baby grand piano in the living room displaying a photograph of Marlene Dietrich. I expected Bette Davis to come out of one room and Joan Crawford to emerge from another.

"I was Marlene's musical director for several years," Burt told me.

He played a few chords at the piano. He hummed a melody and asked me to sing along. The melody was pretty and soon I was singing it full out. One tune led to another. A couple of hours passed while Burt played and I sang. I had a ball.

"I think I can use you as a backup singer with the Girls," he said. "Or maybe even do some solo things with you. You have a fine voice, Carl."

He shook my hand, and I walked out onto Sutton Place on cloud nine. Music carried me all the way as I drifted down the island of Manhattan back to the Village. I told all my friends that Burt Bacharach had discovered me. Everyone was happy for me, but no one was surprised when three or four weeks had passed and I hadn't heard back from Burt.

"Doesn't mean a thing, Baby Boy," said Jackie Verdell. "That's just the music business. He might call you tomorrow, or he might never call. You can't take it personally."

"Why not?" I asked.

"Because Burt Bacharach is hustling like everyone else. He's trying to write another hit for Dionne. Or maybe he's found another Dionne. Or maybe some other big star called, asking him to produce her. You never know. That's the way it is."

"He told me that he liked my voice."

"I'm sure he likes your voice," said Jackie. "Who wouldn't like your voice? But there are hundreds of voices he hears every week."

"He told me he'd help me."

"I'm sure he meant it at the time. But those guys get distracted. It don't mean a thing."

A couple of months later I was asked to audition for the famous producers Hugo and Luigi, who were responsible for a slew of major hits for everyone from Perry Como to the Isley Brothers and Sam Cooke. They had an exclusive deal with RCA records. After receiving good reports about me from other writers and producers, they called me to their Brill Building offices. They had a couple of songs they wanted me to sing.

"Beautiful," said Hugo when I finished.

"Great," said Luigi. "We'll get back to you."

They never did. But I had begun to understand what Jackie Verdell was talking about. That was the music business. Meanwhile, I was still a Gospel Wonder with gigs all over town. Estelle was now an official part of the otherwise all-male group. She and I spent lots of time walking through Harlem, window-shopping and people-watching. We were eating lunch at a small café on St. Nicholas Avenue when she said something that surprised me.

"I'm getting tired of the Wonders."

"How come?" I asked.

"Calvin's cool, but Calvin doesn't know how to follow up with another hit. We need another 'As Long As I've Got Jesus.' How long can you work one song?"

"I'm frustrated too," I said. "The Wonders never gig outside New York."

"Calvin's doing his business thing all day. He's a keypunch operator. That's how he makes his real money. Gospel music is just an aside. I'm getting more work with the Girls than I get with the Wonders."

"Why can't you just keep on doing both?"

"Jerry Wexler has been talking to Cissy. He's so crazy about the way we've been singing behind Aretha, he wants to give us a deal. Cissy is talking about us being a stand-alone group. We even got a new name, not just the Girls, but the Sweet Inspirations. We'll get to make our own records."

"Like the Supremes?"

"Better than the Supremes. We can outsing the Supremes any day of the week."

"You got that right."

"But that means quitting the Wonders."

"I'd hate that, Estelle. I'd hate for us to go on without you."

"Believe me, Baby Boy, that group isn't going anyplace anyway. You need to get out yourself. You need to do better than the Gospel Wonders."

Next thing I knew I was talking to Dee Dee Warwick, who was five years younger than Dionne and a fine singer in her own right. Three years after Dionne had hit big with "Don't Make Me Over" and "Anyone Who Had a Heart," Dee Dee had a hit of her own: "I Want to Be with You." Dionne, the golden girl of the Warwick family, was always generous with her kid sister, but Dee Dee wanted her own career and had a little complex about standing in Dionne's shadow.

"Estelle's quitting the Wonders," I told Dee Dee, "and I've decided to quit along with her. I'd like to go to Chicago. That's where all the big gospel groups are staying. I think I could get hired by a traveling gospel group like the Martin Singers."

"I'm not sure they're hiring," Dee Dee warned me. "You don't want to get stuck up there in cold-ass Chicago without a gig, Baby Boy."

"No, I don't," I confessed.

"Tell you what," she offered. "I'm about to go on tour myself. Why don't you come back to Newark and help me get ready. You can stay upstairs in the room used by Willy, Dionne's valet. You can be my valet. Help me pick out my clothes, make sure my mascara's not running, and go out on the road with me. We'll have a ball. You'll be able to save some money and give yourself some time to see about your next move. What do you say?"

I said yes. We hit the chitlin circuit, where Dee Dee counted on me for more than my valet services. She asked me about vocal interpretations and stage moves. She wanted my opinion about song sequencing. Before she got on stage, she counted on my encouragement. When she got off stage, she needed my assurance that it had all gone well.

In Washington, D.C., we played the Howard Theater along with Billy Stewart. Billy was a big boy with a beautiful high voice and a trademark stutter built into his vocal style. Billy was an original. He recorded for Chess, the label out of Chicago that had blues artists like Muddy Waters and Howlin' Wolf, plus Chuck Berry and Etta James. Billy had four songs that drove the audiences crazy—"I Do Love You," "Sitting in the Park," "Summertime," and a hair-raising cover version of Doris Day's big hit "Secret Love."

In addition to her songs that had climbed up the R & B chart, Dee Dee did a cover that never failed to bring down the house: Leiber and Stoller's "I (Who Have Nothing)." It had been a smash for Ben E. King, but when Dee Dee sang it live, everyone forgot about him. She drained that song dry and had audiences screaming for more.

When we got to the Regal Theater in Chicago, Jackie Verdell reintroduced me to Chuck Jackson, who had enjoyed big hits for Florence Greenberg's Scepter label—"I Don't Want to Cry," "Any Day Now," and "Something You Got." I knew he had been discovered by his idol, Jackie Wilson, and that he'd written with Luther Dixon. I also knew he was a big gospel music man who had sung with the Raymond Raspberry Singers.

"Haven't I heard you with the Wonders?" Chuck asked. "Aren't you the brother with the booming voice?"

I smiled and said yes. "But you guys in the Raspberry Singers," I added, "y'all had the real voices."

Chuck and I started talking about how Raymond Raspberry was the first to infuse an all-men's group with the high harmony of a female group. Beginning as Clara Ward's piano player, he modeled his own sound on a male version of the female Famous Ward Singers. Raspberry turned out to be one of the most prolific gospel writers of all time.

"I'm out there singing this R & B," said Chuck. "But gospel's really where it's at."

Dee Dee happened to overhear Chuck's last remark. "Ain't no better gospel singer than Baby Boy," she said, patting me on the back. "He's just out here making sure my lipstick is on straight. But it won't be long before he gets his big break."

When we arrived in Baltimore for a show at the Royal, it was old home week. My buddies came by Dee Dee's dressing room to see me. My childhood friend Ralph, who had introduced me to gut-bucket gospel, showed up, and I welcomed him with open arms.

"Carl," he said, "this is what New York has taught you? Now you're ironing some lady's dress and shining her shoes?"

"Dee Dee's cool," I said. "She put me right in the middle of that whole Newark thing—with Dionne, Cissy, Estelle, and all the others."

"Yeah, but shouldn't you be singing?"

"Never intend to stop singing. Where are you singing these days, Ralph?"

"Alex Bradford called. He wants me to come to Chicago. He's got a decent local group there, but he's getting ready to go back on the road. He wants to upgrade his group. He's looking for singers. You should come with me, Carl."

"I've made this commitment to Dee Dee. I can't leave her without any help."

The big stop on the tour was the Apollo. We arrived in the theater, where, during our short afternoon rehearsal, Dee Dee seemed lost.

"What's on you mind?" I asked.

"Baby Boy," she said, "when I walk into this place, I can't help but think about Dionne. Were you here when she recently played the Apollo?"

"I was," I said. "She brought downtown uptown, didn't she?"

"She sure enough did," Dee Dee remembered. "She didn't use the house band. She came in with her own orchestra. She had her own staging, and she went through at least four costume changes, wearing one gorgeous gown after another. It was something to see."

Dee Dee sighed. It wasn't hard to read her mind.

"Well, Dionne has a beautiful voice," I said, "and it's wonderful how Bacharach hooked her up with Ed Sullivan and got her all those movie theme songs. Dionne has been blessed, but so have you, Dee Dee. When you break into 'I (Who Have Nothing),' there's no singer out there—in Hollywood, California; Las Vegas, Nevada; or Newark, New Jersey—who can touch you."

"I love me some Baby Boy," she said, kissing me on the cheek.

Dee Dee had a good week at the Apollo, but my mind was back in Baltimore, going over my discussion with Ralph. What was I doing sitting in the wings? Why wasn't I out there singing? As I watched the lead singers for the male groups, I noticed how hard they tried to excite that hard-to-please Apollo audience. They fell on their knees, they switched to falsetto, they fondled the mic, they swiveled their hips like strippers, but mostly the crowd yawned. But I knew the crowd responded to strong voices and that if I could get out there, I'd cause a riot. And I wasn't the only one who felt that way. Dee Dee was always bragging on me. Estelle never tired of praising me. And so did the one we all considered the best—Jackie Verdell. "I don't care nothing about no Brook Benton or Walter Jackson," Jackie liked to say. "Baby Boy, you can blow 'em all away." She was my biggest booster.

So what was Baby Boy doing in the wings? Getting ready to roll out on his own.

TOO CLOSE TO HEAVEN

It was deep winter, and I was living in East Orange, New Jersey. As much as I loved Dee Dee, I was tired of picking out her scarves and zipping up her gowns. I was tired of *not* singing, *not* performing, *not* expressing the musical joy that was so deeply a part of me. My energy could no longer be contained. Newark had been great. I had fallen in love with the turkey-and-Russian-dressing rye bread sandwiches at Peterman's Deli. Dee Dee had been wonderful to me. The Sweet Inspirations—Cissy, Estelle, Sylvia, and Myrna—had become my sisters. They were the hottest background group in the country. When Aretha wasn't using them, Barbra Streisand, Connie Francis, Neil Diamond, and Elvis Presley were. They brought me along for an occasional session, but most of their gigs did not require a male voice. And no matter how close our bond, we would never be the Sweet Inspirations Plus Baby Boy.

I had to get out, and I figured that Chicago was the place. It was still the center of the gospel universe, and my friend Ralph was there, having hooked up with Alex Bradford.

I was too broke to buy a bus ticket, so I hitchhiked. On the morning I left, snow was falling hard. I must have been crazy. Why else would I walk through the storm, all the way from East Orange to the New Jersey Turnpike? Why else would I stick out my thumb and, with a short prayer to God, stand in the freezing cold until a carload of guys picked me up?

They were white boys heading to Chicago and happy to take me along. They were eager to talk black and show off their liberalism, and I was happy to give them all the validation they needed. They were also especially macho. So there I was, this little queen, talkin' 'bout girls' boobs and booties. I became one of the guys. Meanwhile, they took a liking to me, and by the time we reached the Windy City, they gave me fifty dollars to help tide me over. Thank God for those guys.

Ralph had told me that Alex Bradford stayed at the Gramiere, a residential hotel, and I found my way over there. The desk clerk said that Professor Bradford was out but could be reached by phone. I immediately called him up.

"Who is this?" asked Alex.

"Carl Bean."

"What are you doing in Chicago, Carl?"

I paused before answering. I didn't want to tell Alex that Ralph had tipped me off to the fact that he was forming a new group for the road. In fact, Ralph and I decided it'd be better if Alex didn't even know we were childhood friends.

"I want to get into big-time gospel," I told him, "and Chicago is the place. I figured I'd try out for the Martin Singers."

"Well, listen here, Carl, you stay where you are in that lobby. I'll be back in a couple of hours and we'll talk then."

That's when I knew that Alex had remembered my voice. He knew I could sing. When he arrived at the hotel, he invited me up to the apartment that he shared with his wife.

"You have a place to stay in Chicago?" he asked.

"I don't," I said, "but if you let me clean up, do the dishes, and make the beds around here, I'd be grateful to sleep on your couch."

Alex laughed. "You'd do anything to stay in Chicago, wouldn't you?"

"Anything."

"Well, let's give it a try."

During these first days in Chicago, I kept Bradford's place spotless. He went about his business, making phone calls, answering his mail, taking his meals. The minute he was through eating, I'd whisk away his plate, scrub it clean, and serve him coffee. I also spent a great deal of time observing him. He was a character of the highest order, nonstop energy and sharp as a tack. He could talk like a street cat or university scholar; he could wear out any piano or Hammond B-3; he could whip up a song—gospel, gut-bucket blues, or fiery R & B; he could orchestrate a mass choir of eighty or a small group of six. And to top it all off, the man could sing. The man could wail. He had one of the great gospel voices of his or any era.

Bradford was born in Bessemer, Alabama, and still bore traces of his country church upbringing. But he was also big-city smart and big-city slick. Alex was no one's fool. He had not only revolutionized gospel singing with a down-home approach that made him Ray Charles's favorite, he had built up a business—recording, music publishing, and touring—that he and his wife, Alberta, ran with an iron fist. Alex loved to talk about his fellow Alabaman, the man they called Prophet Jones, who also hailed from Bessemer. Jones had founded the Universal Triumph/Dominion of God Church in Detroit, which Bradford had attended as a teenager. Services were held in the Oriole Theater, and he described the Prophet's style of preaching and living as the most glorious he had ever witnessed.

"The man had a mansion of fifty-four rooms," Alex told me. "He had a dozen servants and a half-dozen Cadillacs. He wore robes of Russian sable and sat in a gold throne that he claimed was from King Solomon. When he was through with his sermon, I saw women throw down their white minks for him to walk on. Prophet Jones was spectacular."

Alex Bradford knew how to make a production out of a sacred singing service. Yet he could never escape his effeminacy.

He was a queen, and the gospel world knew it. His peers called him Miss Bradford. His nickname was Pearl. Despite his marriage, no one doubted that he was attracted to men.

Alex was also deeply insecure. He had a peculiar face, fatter on the bottom than on top. Throughout his life, he told a story about how, at age thirteen, he had barely escaped a deadly encounter when the owner of the drugstore where he worked went after him for calling a white female customer by her first name. Fearing for her son's life, Alex's mom sent him off to New York. Such early traumas took their toll.

By the time I met him, Alex had developed into a diva. In fact, Ralph suggested that I not ask him for a job.

"He's the kind of guy who would prefer to initiate the process. He wants to feel that he discovered you," he explained.

So I kept up the ruse that my chief aim was to audition for the Martin Singers.

After a week or so, I was cleaning up the apartment when Alex said he had to go out. "Alberta," he told his wife, "you rehearse the group when they get here."

Alberta was a superb piano player who had played for Marion Williams and the Stars of Faith, the unit that had broken away from Clara Ward. When the other singers arrived—my secret friend Ralph, Bobby Hill, Charles Campbell, and Kenneth Rayborn, who sang and also played piano—Alberta began the rehearsal. Before they could really get started, the phone rang. It was Alex. When their brief conversation was over, Alberta said, "Carl, Alex wants to see if you can handle his second lead."

I did so effortlessly. The harmony between me and Ralph was pitch-perfect, a family harmony, like the Staples had.

Alberta, a Baltimorean like us, was no one's fool. "Y'all are both from Baltimore," she said, "you're singing like you've been together your whole life, and you're telling me that you've never met until today?"

She gave us this who-you-kidding look that nearly cracked us up, but we managed to keep a straight face. We didn't want to do anything to mess up my chance of getting hired. By the time Alex got home, we had it all together.

"This is your new group to take on the road," Alberta announced to him. "Ain't gonna get no better than this."

Alex asked us to sing the songs we'd been rehearsing. He scrutinized us like crazy. Fortunately, we avoided any mistakes. Next thing I knew, we were on the road.

In Philly, we appeared at the Met, a glorious old opera house used for big-time gospel revues. All of black Philly was coming out. Back in the dressing rooms, I got glimpses of the Caravans, the Soul Stirrers, and the Ward Singers. I was sharing the stage with the best singers in the land, the most loved and respected of all the groups. They were also the highest paid. Our pay was minimal. Alex was pocketing most of the money, but I was too new to challenge him—and too scared.

Sometimes fear is a good motivator. In this case, it kept me on the straight and narrow. I never missed rehearsals or abused my instrument. I made sure to get to the gigs early. My one ambition was to be a gospel singer capable of standing toe-to-toe with the Sallie Martin Singers and the Five Blind Boys of Alabama. Alex afforded me this chance, and I wasn't about to mess it up. Alex took us into every major gospel venue in the country, including Madison Square Garden, where we performed at the Miss Black America pageant.

One of our singers, Charles Campbell, was always in the company of his partner Smitty. In the closeted gay world of gospel, Charles and Smitty were the only openly homosexual couple I knew and a model of domestic happiness, a couple for whom same-sex attraction involved more than flesh. They demonstrated companionship, caring, and devotion. Unlike Alex, Charles was sober and clearheaded. Like my mentor Reverend O'Neill, he came out of Clarence Cobbs's First Church of Deliverance in Chicago, and consequently had a progressive theology and a wholeness of thought. In public, Charles and Smitty were openly affectionate, eager to show the world that the bond between them was more than friendship; it was romantic love. The men remained partners for some forty years. Our paths would cross again. But meeting the two of them, especially during my rookie days on the major league gospel circuit, brought a balance to the crazy world I was now a part of.

Being a Bradford Singer changed my life in profound ways. Because of our vibrantly colorful robes and extravagant vocal style, we were considered the most flamboyant group in all gospel, a label we embraced with pride. When we called each other "Miss Carl" or "Miss Charles" or "Miss Bradford," we did so affectionately. Those terms of endearment carried positive connotations. We had style, we had talent, we had extroverted personalities, and we didn't mind showing off a bit.

As Ray Charles once observed, gospel folks party harder than anyone. I watched from afar. I did so because I was, in essence, still Baby Boy. My elders were protective of me. During the grueling tours, if I had time to spare, I gravitated toward people interested in the political and artistic world around them.

The touring world was new to me. In Philly, for example, we stayed at the home of Nina, a famous hostess in black music culture. Nina had a sprawling house—today you'd call it a bed-and-breakfast—and catered to entertainers. She invited you to select your own pork chops or pigs' ears from her freezer. Then she cooked them for you in nothing flat. She also served orange juice and vodka all day long. Meanwhile, the local boosters came by with stolen goods. Her guests could buy flashy suits or fine Borsalino fedoras at bargain-basement prices.

The trips through the South were scary. Once we made a wrong turn onto the private property of a crazed white man, and he unleashed a half-dozen killer Dobermans. We barely escaped. The highway patrol harassed us continually. When we wouldn't pay their bribes, they threw us in jail. Countless restaurants in Mississippi or Georgia refused us a plain glass of water. Tensions were high. Murder was in the air.

When we got to Birmingham, Alex's home territory, we checked into the A. G. Gaston Motel. Mr. Gaston was a black entrepreneur who also owned the funeral home. He showed us the room where Dr. King had once stayed. Then he took us around the corner to the Sixteenth Street Baptist Church, where on September 15, 1963, Carol Denise McNair, eleven, Cynthia Diane Wesley, fourteen, Carole Rosamond Robertson, fourteen, and Addie Mae Collins, fourteen, were killed by a terrorist bomb set by the Ku Klux Klan. We stood there for a long time and wept.

Alex took me to the graveyard where his mom and dad were buried. He sobbed like a baby.

"Baby Boy," he said, tears flooding his face, "Mama was a cook, a hairdresser, and an insurance agent. She was a woman who made something of her life. She was the woman who made me."

Sometimes we stayed with Alex's sister, Ophelia, who ran an after-hours joint in her home and sold corn whisky off the back porch.

After a week or two on the road, we'd find ourselves back in Chicago's Gramiere Hotel. That's where I saw a different side of Alex. He had written a song called "Never Ever" in an up-tempo shoutin' rhythm. I heard it differently. When Alex took a break from the piano, I had Kenneth play the song, suggesting we slow it down to a crawl. As I sang it, I started to feel the influence of the ladies who had formed my vocal style. I thought of the Divine One, Sarah Vaughan, and my dear sister Jackie Verdell, the most jazzlike of all gospel singers. I even thought of Rosemary Clooney and Doris Day, whose voices had been inside my head ever since I was a child. I sang Alex's song like a bluesy jazz ballad. Hearing my interpretation, Alex jumped up from the couch and got right in my face.

"That's horrible!" he screamed. "That's the worst thing I've ever heard. You don't understand the song. You ruined the song. You turned it into something it's not. Who do you think you are, Nancy Wilson? If you were ever stupid enough to sing anything like this in a black church, they'd throw you out on your ear!"

I wanted to say that Jackie Verdell sang like that all the time and had never been thrown out of a black church, but I kept quiet. While Alex was throwing his fit, the other Bradford singers kept their eyes glued to the floor.

We thought the storm had passed, but later that summer his mood turned dark again. We were in St. Louis, in the midst of a heat wave, and Alex was furious that we hadn't rehearsed. Our rationale was that it was 100 degrees and we needed to conserve our energy for the service/concert that night. Alex was inconsolable. "Y'all are just trying to get out of work," he said. The evening service was held in one of the biggest black churches in the city, and the music royalty was out in force. Sitting on the first pew were the O'Neal Twins, famous for songs like "I'd Trade a Lifetime" and "I've Decided to Follow Jesus," and Willie Mae Ford Smith, the woman gospel fans called Mother. Willie Mae was the mentor of Brother Joe May and a towering figure in the midwestern music scene. Her big hit, "If You Just Keep Still," was a classic.

When it was time for our first number, Alex pulled a surprise. He went to the mic and said, "You know, folks, singers can get a little lazy. And my singers got especially lazy today when they decided not to rehearse. So rather than try any new material on you, I'm going to have to go back to my tried-and-true songs that you know so well."

Well, Alex was right, we had been singing *only* new material, but we didn't know the tried-and-true songs. We tried to fake it, but our performance turned out disastrously.

"You can see that these fools up in here don't even know the old songs," said Alex, "so I guess I'm going to have to let them sing individually for you. Since they're so determined not to listen to their leader, let's see what they can do on their own."

Ralph and Bobby started off doing solo numbers they'd done many times before. I didn't know any solo numbers. I panicked. All I could think of was "Never Ever," the song I had sung in Chicago when Kenneth had accompanied me on piano. The only way I sang it was in that slow, jazz-infused style that I liked and Alex hated. So I bent, caressed, elongated, and punctuated the lyrics, adorning them with swooping phrases; I attacked one note; I bit off the next. I laid out the song in a manner that expressed my excitement, my love of the Lord, and my appreciation of secular singers like Ella Fitzgerald and Carmen McRae. In my mind, I saw no division between religious and worldly. It was all Jesus' music, all born from the goodness of Christ.

Well, the thing tore the house down. I mean *Tore. It. Down.* The church exploded. Both O'Neal Twins got up and started shouting, "Sing it! You sing it, son!" Mother Smith was screaming, "Glory! Glory to God!" I started walking the aisles while people reached out to touch my robe and encourage me to keep on keeping on. Alex was shocked, but as a pro, he was always calculating the audience's reaction. So in the middle of the number, he pushed Kenneth aside and accompanied me himself, playing in the slow style he had found so repugnant. He laid down beautiful chord progressions that had jazz written all over them.

When the concert was over, Alex didn't say a word to me. He acted like everything was fine. And in fact, from then on, we performed a version of "Never Ever" in my slowed-down, jazzed-up style every night. Soon Alex was talking like the crowd-pleasing version had been his invention all along. I didn't care. I got to sing, and the saints got to praise God.

EARTH MOTHER

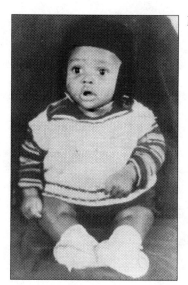

My family's earliest photo of me.

My natural mother, Arlene, in her early twenties. She inscribed this picture to me when I was in elementary school.

My beautiful godmother, Jeter, the woman I called Mom.

Age ten, when I was in the fourth grade in 1954.

My godfather, Harry, truly a great provider and a loving dad.

My best friend Rex in our backyard. I confided in him night and day.

Reverend Marcus Garvey Wood of Baltimore's Providence Baptist Church. He remains the single most influential minister in my walk with Christ. I encountered his loving teachings as a child, and, a half century later, I remain his disciple. *(Courtesy of the Providence Baptist Church)*

The great Professor Alex Bradford, one of the most brilliant artists in the history of our music and the man who brought me into the gospel major leagues. *(Courtesy of Concord Music Group)*

Vinnette Justine Carroll: wonderful artist, writer, actress, director, producer, visionary—and beloved mentor. (*Photographs and Prints Division, Schomburg Center for Research in Black Culture, The New York Public Library, Astor, Lenox and Tilden Foundations*)

Miss Lillie Jackson, "the Mother of Freedom," president of the Baltimore NAACP from 1947–1970, and an inspiration who changed the course of my life. (*Courtesy of the Afro-American Newspapers*)

In New York City in 1962. At eighteen, I was on my own, working at Macy's, and discovering the gospel world of Harlem.

My sister Martha, pregnant with her daughter Carla. Baltimore, 1956.

1971. The original caption for the photo showing a workshop version of
"Don't Bother Me, I Can't Cope": "Alan Weeks holding Glory Van Scott,
Bradford Singers l to r, Kenneth Rayborn, Carl Bean, Bobby Hill, and
Prof. Alex Bradford rehearse the "Can't No Grave Hold My Body Down"
number in "Don't Bother Me, I Can't Cope," a new revue Vinnette
Carroll's Urban Arts Corps will perform on a city-wide tour . . . kick-off
at Lincoln Center Library and Museum for the Performing Arts."

Universal Love, 1974. Left to right, Craig Harris, Royal Anderson, Alvin Cannon, and Alejandro Romeo. That's me, chin in hand.

Motown publicity photo, 1977. I'm getting ready to go out and tour behind "I Was Born This Way."

In the eighties, when the church was still meeting at the Ebony Showcase, one of our talented members, R. Steele, drew this beautiful androgynous face that became a part of our logo.

With singer Nancy Wilson. Nancy was one of the first people to contact me about my AIDS work and to offer her help. She sang at our AIDS fundraiser, "Coming Home for Friends," at the Shrine Auditorium in Los Angeles.

With U.S. Representative Maxine Waters and Dionne Warwick at the Shrine Auditorium. Both Maxine and Dionne have been strong supporters of our AIDS ministry. I have been a family friend of the Warwicks since my years in Newark in the 1960s. Dionne has been an angel; her early support made the Shrine fundraisers successful.

The irony was this: I moved out of Newark to get into the gospel world of Chicago. Then in the midsixties, only months after I joined Alex Bradford, he was reappointed minister of music at Newark's Greater Abyssinian Church and moved us back east with him. Thus I was right back where I started. Newark, though, was fine with me because it meant working with the Bradford Singers *and* the Abyssinian choir that Alex led.

Abyssinian's constituency was largely transplanted southerners. The church had a warm down-home feel and its members embraced me from the very first day. I loved that southern comfort, the welcoming greeting of "Come on over, we're having dinner right after services and you are surely welcome." It reminded me of my mother's mom, Nana, who had loved me so mightily.

One afternoon, Alex brought me and his other singers to New York City to meet Vinnette Justine Carroll, a woman of the theater. She was also an artist of wondrous creativity who played a major role in the development of African American culture. Both sophisticated and wise, she touched the hearts of her students and changed their lives. I was blessed to be one of them. A big-boned woman, she wore dramatic silver cuff bracelets and large stone rings. She dressed in fabulous African clothes imported from Nairobi and colorful woven scarves bought from sidewalk vendors in Greenwich Village. At work she wore jeans, sneakers and T-shirts. She had been raised in Jamaica and on Strivers' Row in Harlem, the architecturally distinguished district where W. C. Handy, the blues pioneer, and Fletcher Henderson, the musician, had lived.

Vinnette had several graduate degrees and had worked as a psychologist before turning to the theater. She had studied acting with Lee Strasberg and Stella Adler and had developed a one-woman show that she took on the road. She won an Obie for her role in *Moon on a Rainbow Shawl* and an Emmy for *Beyond the Blues,* her tribute to black poetry. Working with Langston Hughes and Alex, she also created *Black Nativity,* a successful merging of gospel music and theatrical storytelling.

Vinnette was a writer, director, and producer but, above all, a teacher. Her mission was to introduce black kids to black culture—paintings and plays, dance and poetry, songs and musicals—that she loved so passionately.

My relationship with Vinnette began when she was in her forties and I was in my early twenties. When Alex introduced us, she immediately recruited the Bradford Singers into her Urban Arts Corps, which she had recently founded. The purpose of the Corps was to train young black performers in the techniques of theater—acting, directing, writing, staging, and lighting. She saw the field as an organic whole. Poetry related to jazz, just as jazz related to theater, just as gospel related to jazz. She had no prejudices about genre and thought outside restrictive categories.

"It's all art," Vinnette liked to say, "and we're all artists. We can write, we can sing, we can dance. We come out of different traditions, but we need not stay in our separate rooms. We can all come together, combine, share, and, in doing so, create something glorious and new."

If Alex had been my mentor in Chicago, Vinnette was my new mentor in New York. My relationship with Vinnette grew closer as my relationship with Alex grew strained. At Greater

Abyssinian in Newark, when the saints cheered my version of "Never Ever," Alex made snide remarks, indicating his envy. Increasingly, he grew cold and hostile.

In contrast, Vinnette was supportive and warm. Every week I took the train from Newark to Manhattan, jumped on the subway, got off at Union Square, walked by the S. Klein department store, and headed over to Twentieth Street, where her Urban Arts Corps was housed in a huge space in an office building. I opened the huge silver art deco door with UAC written in bold letters and was immediately in the world of high drama.

Vinnette was 100 percent greasepaint. When she wasn't training us to perform in a formal production, she gave us vignettes to read. She coached us in dramatic monologues, in the formal reading of poetry, and, of course, in the interpretation of plays. She taught us how to stand on stage, how to project, how to enunciate, how to bring a character to life. Vinnette was also an artistic entrepreneur. She was always putting something together. With a grant from the New York State Council for the Arts, we did *Dark of the Moon,* a bizarre hillbilly play, at the State University of New York at Brockport. Alex wrote the music and we tutored the senior theater and dance students. We also played the parts of warlocks, faeries, and spirits. It was wild and wonderful.

Vinnette brought me to the center of the avant-garde cultural life of New York City. We caught glimpses of her friends Harry Belafonte, Sidney Poitier, and James Baldwin. Cicely Tyson actually did a workshop with us. We worked on *When Hell Freezes Over, I'll Skate,* Vinnette's play inspired by the poetry of Langston Hughes and Paul Lawrence Dunbar. Ms. Tyson instructed us in the art of phrasing, elocution, and dramatic gesticulation. "Make certain your heart understands these words," she said, "before your mouth speaks them."

On Vinnette's recommendation, I read, among others, Amiri

Baraka, Gwendolyn Brooks, and Malcolm X. She took me to the New School, where we heard lectures on black dance presentations by George Faison, Talley Beatty, and Louis Johnson. Just as Reverend Marcus Garvey Wood at the Providence Baptist had opened my eyes to socially conscious Christianity, Vinnette opened my mind to the world of ideas and creativity. Thanks to Vinnette, I wound up with what amounted to a well-rounded education in the arts.

As the old folk say in church, "God may not be there when you want him, but he's always right on time." Vinnette's appearance in my life was also right on time. She pushed Baby Boy in a way that no one had pushed him before. She took Baby Boy—as well as Alex and the other Bradford Singers—and changed our direction.

"Become permanent members of the Urban Arts Corps," she said. "Work with me every day. Let's create projects together. Let's marry gospel music and the legitimate theater. Let's keep the spirit—the faith, the hope, and the beauty of great gospel— and inject it with stories that everyone can relate to. Robes are beautiful, and robes have a beautiful place in gospel choirs, but let's take off those robes and wear the clothes of ordinary people—suits and ties, skirts and blouses—and still project the force of sacred music. Let's become actors. Let's create plays. Let's create musicals. Let's do everything we can to infuse the natural theatricality of gospel into works that we can present on stages all over this country. Let's take those works to the world. What do you say?"

Alex said yes. We said yes. And with that, Vinnette began developing two musicals. The first, *Don't Bother Me, I Can't Cope*, was written by Micki Grant, a fabulous singer, composer, and close associate of Vinnette's. She was also a superb actress and was, in fact, the first African American cast member of a daytime soap opera, *Another World*. The second musical, *Your Arms Too*

Short to Box with God, based on the Book of Matthew, was a collaboration between Alex, Micki, and Vinnette.

Vinnette won a Tony nomination for best director for *Arms,* making her the first black woman to receive that honor. Touring companies for both shows traveled the world over. They created stars: Hope Clarke, later of Alvin Ailey's celebrated company, came out of *Cope,* and Jennifer Holliday, who would later star as Effie in *Dreamgirls,* came out of *Arms.* Before these triumphs came years of hard work. It was more than breaking down the line between gospel music and musical comedy; it was teaching us choir kids how to move, project, and act on stage.

Naturally, I was thrilled. As a little boy pretending to be Ethel Merman, I had dreamed of playing Broadway. Now I was heading in that very direction. Giving up touring on the gospel circuit was an easy adjustment. The travel had already grown tedious, and there was nothing I wanted to do more than work with Vinnette. In both productions, the musical vignettes and slices of black life were compelling. The song titles said it all—"I Gotta Keep Movin'," "Harlem Streets," "Good Vibrations," "It Takes a Whole Lot of Human Feeling," "We're Gonna Have a Good Time," "Judas Dance," "When the Power Comes," "I Love You So Much, Jesus."

Vinnette was always concerned with our financial welfare. She paid us generously. During the winter holidays she found venues—a church or school auditorium—for us to perform *Black Nativity.* For one of these performances, we were warming up when Alex heard me singing "Mary, Don't You Weep." Because I was singing it so dramatically, he went ballistic. He accused me of showing off. "The *B* in this group is for *Bradford,*" Alex shouted, "not *Bean!*" His tirade brought us all down. Increasingly, Alex's ego was getting to be a problem.

At the start of my work with the Urban Arts Corps, I was still staying at Alex's with the other Bradford Singers in Newark. His house was a safe haven, a replica of family life. Alex acted as our daddy. He paid the rent and fed us dinner. He might have been jealous of my talent, but he was my main provider. We didn't quite realize that we were underpaid for our services until Vinnette insisted that we join the union, which made us eligible to work at Equity theaters. Alex was against a minimum pay scale; he didn't think we deserved any employee rights. But Vinnette was stronger than Alex and insisted that the old paternalistic paradigm be replaced by a system of accountability. She made sure we worked under our own name.

Meanwhile, Alex's home in Newark began to lose its sense of stability. There was lots of liquor and gambling. Getting high became the norm. I didn't fight that program; I went along with it, although I knew my clarity was quickly slipping away. At one point, though, I decided to take a break from the boozy environment and enrolled at a Bible college in New Jersey. My experience at Providence Baptist in Baltimore had never left my heart, and I felt like I needed to recharge my spiritual batteries. Unfortunately, the charger was defective.

The school, largely white, was racist. They had one scholarship student, a brother from Sierra Leone, mopping the floors, taking out the trash, and living apart from the whites. My best friend was a white girl with a keen interest in theology. She and I spent long evenings discussing the Bible. Our relationship was completely platonic, but when the administrators saw us together, they threatened to expel us if we didn't end it. When the dean's son, a pretty white boy, showed up in my dorm room in nothing but his scanty briefs, I knew it was time to hightail it out of there. After two months, I went back to Newark, reestablished myself at Alex's house, and rejoined the Corps.

"Leave Newark, Carl," said Vinnette at one point. "You'll do better if you get out from under Alex's thumb."

"Where would I go?"

"The city. You need to be in Manhattan, Baby Boy. Find yourself a little place up in Harlem where rents are low and energy is high."

"Where am I going to get the money?"

"I'll loan you a little."

I took the leap and moved into a little place on St. Nicholas. I was happy to be away from Alex's place, yet the lack of a home had an unexpected impact on me. For years, the gospel world, for all its dysfunctional aspects, had been my family. We all lived together in a big house. When we were on the road, we stayed together, ate together, prayed together, performed together. Then, just like that, I was alone. I didn't like that feeling of isolation and sought ways to change it. Promiscuous sex, though, only made the loneliness worse. Such encounters distracted me from facing things I didn't want to face. In truth, companionship is what I sought, but sex is all I got. I was becoming addicted to anonymous sex.

All this came in the midst of the political turmoil of the sixties. When the news of the assassination of Martin Luther King Jr. came over the radio on April 4, 1968, I couldn't stay in my apartment on 158th Street and St. Nicholas Avenue. I had to be out on the city streets, distracted by the traffic and passing crowds. Pain consumed me, but I wasn't surprised or shocked by the news itself. After all, in the movement back in Baltimore, I had heard countless stories of men who had been murdered or whose homes had been bombed. The incidents of brutality were commonplace. As a young man, I had been taught about sacrificial love. I had learned that to liberate a people, blood had to be shed. I had been trained to believe that white rage and fear would inevitably lead to violence, but that the violence could not be resisted. It had to be absorbed, and Martin had absorbed it.

As I reached Central Park, it seemed strange that on this day, life on earth was continuing as though nothing had happened. *Christ is the living example of the principle of salvation*, I thought to myself. *But now it seems that still another crucifixion is needed, another follower of Christ must fall so that we may be free.* It was a horrific formula. Yet when a voice cries out against the ruling class, this is what happens.

As I left the park and headed downtown, I kept thinking that it was one thing for Martin to be working for black civil rights. But when he began his poor people's campaign and embraced the disenfranchised of every race—coal miners in West Virginia, factory workers in Pennsylvania, garbage collectors in Memphis—he threatened those in power. When he spread out beyond racial issues and attacked the senseless war in Vietnam, that was too much for America to bear. He had to go.

I had to sing. In Midtown, in the midst of shoppers carrying bags from Saks and Bergdorf Goodman, I sang "Precious Lord, Take My Hand." I sang "Oh, Freedom." Singing has always been my balm, melodies my medicine against the heartless cruelty of a cold world. I sang because I needed to communicate with God. The world was messed up. God was not. The world slays leaders who seek radical change based on universal love and universal acceptance. And the world had slain them—Christ, Gandhi, and now Martin.

Fear ruled in the world's kingdom.

Love ruled in God's kingdom.

And though the songs I sang brought me comfort, the tension between these two worlds—one fueled by fright, the other by faith—was excruciating. Across America, black communities exploded.

We pressed on. God used my talents to help me cope with my pain. And God blessed Vinnette, who had us working all the time. We tightened *Don't Bother Me, I Can't Cope* in out-of-town venues. We took the show to Philly, then to Detroit, where we shared a residential hotel with members of the Ice Capades. That really made me feel like I was in show business. At Ford's Theater in D.C., where Lincoln had been shot, the show came together. Our next step was off-Broadway, and then Broadway itself.

My sex addiction deepened. Most of the time I was a conscientious member of the troupe. At rehearsals, I took Vinnette's direction to heart and was the first to arrive and the last to leave. But there were also times when my compulsive behavior of sex for sex's sake got the best of me. I binged. I went to the baths, where anonymous encounters were the norm. I would cruise the bars, where I would pick up a guy, take him back to my place, have sex, and then, an hour or so later, find myself back in that same spot looking to score again. Once this happened nine or ten times in the same day. It was crazy. And I wasn't alone in my craziness. So many in New York were living the promiscuous life that the health department showed up at choir rehearsal and announced an outbreak of syphilis. Some cases had been traced back to specific schools and congregations. We were given blood tests and told to take precautions.

I was also still smoking weed and drinking wine, but the core addiction was indiscriminate sex, meaningless sex, sex without heart, sex for sex's sake. The high was the mere sight of a willing stranger and physical contact divorced of anything personal. The high was physical contact resulting in ejaculation. I knew what I was doing: I was trying to fix something by making it even worse. As a molested child, I had been objectified, and as an adult, I was compulsively continuing the pattern by objectifying myself and others.

Ultimately, the lessons learned at Providence Baptist were too strong to be ignored, even in the midst of my crazy addiction. I had been taught to uplift my race. I had been taught that social responsibility was a key to spiritual growth; Christ's lesson was to love others as he loves us. Love had nothing to do with my sexual escapades. I was not loving others, I was using others, and

I got sick of it. I was covered with shame. My life was leading nowhere. I needed something else.

But even when I came to the theater after a binge of too much sex, too many Kool cigarettes, and too many joints, my head cloudy and my performance subpar, Vinnette never gave up on me. She said, "Baby Boy, you're having a bad day. Try to focus and try to be present. I know you can do it. Just clear out the cobwebs and bring yourself to this song. Project it. Deliver it. Make it come alive." Her words pierced through my fog and I responded to her encouragement.

At the same time, Alex was manipulating me. At times, he praised my work. Other times, feeling upstaged, he gave me the cold shoulder. The love/hate vibe was powerful and confusing. It went on for years and came to a sad climax.

Cope was selling out off-Broadway and we were almost ready for its Broadway debut.

"Sure, business is brisk," said Alex, "but Vinnette isn't paying us our fair share."

"That doesn't sound like Vinnette," I told Alex. "I've never seen her be anything *but* fair."

"You don't know her like I do," Alex replied. "I've been working with her for over a decade. She's talented, she's driven, but she's funny with money. That's why the other singers and I have decided to boycott the big performance Saturday night. We need to show her that we mean business. We need a raise."

"So we're just going to leave her in the lurch?"

"There's no other way," said Alex. "Don't show up Saturday."

"I hate to do that to Vinnette," I said.

"You'll hate it worse if me and the rest of the company look at you like a scab."

I didn't want to be seen as a scab, so I didn't go to the theater that Saturday night. On Monday morning, when I arrived bright and early at the Urban Arts Corps, Vinnette came up to me.

"Baby Boy, are you all right? Did you get sick or something?"

"What do you mean?" I asked.

"You didn't show Saturday night. We had to replace you for the performance."

"I didn't think there would be a performance," I explained. "Alex said we were boycotting. He said that was the only way to get you to give us a raise."

"What!" Vinnette exclaimed. "Alex Bradford is crazy! He was there Saturday, and so were all the other singers. He was just straight-up lying to you, Baby Boy, 'cause he didn't like how the crowds have been giving you standing ovations."

Something snapped in me. I loved Alex Bradford's talent. I recognized him as gospel royalty, but given his lying and manipulating ways, I now saw him as gospel garbage.

"Who you calling gospel garbage?" Alex screamed when I confronted him.

"You. You tried to get me on the wrong side of Vinnette. You're consumed with jealousy. You're a backbiter and you're a liar and I can't stand being in your presence for a minute more."

"Look here, Carl Bean. I pay you a dollar to holler. If you don't want my dollar, go holler somewhere else."

"You don't pay me, Vinnette does."

"Without me, Vinnette wouldn't have this big-time success. Everyone knows that. Even Vinnette."

"You tried to turn Vinnette against me."

"Look here, Vinnette's got no more use for you. Vinnette's tired of your grandstanding, and so is everyone else."

"Vinnette loves me. Vinnette told me that I have the talent to make it. Vinnette's the one who said I'm a blessing to you."

"Don't make me laugh," said Alex. "If Vinnette has to choose between you and me, who do you think she's gonna pick—the headliner who's writing her songs, or some backup singer?"

"I don't want to put her in that position," I said.

"She's already in that position. She's got no time for you and all your whining. No one does."

"I'm not whining. I'm just saying that you've been dirty-dealing with me and all the other singers from the get-go."

"You ain't thinking right."

"I'm thinking that the further away I get from you, Alex Bradford, the happier I'll be."

"We're taking *Cope* to Broadway," Alex reminded me. "You've been talking 'bout playing Broadway ever since I've known you. So I don't believe you, Baby Boy—not for a single minute. You ain't walking. No one walks out on a chance to perform on Broadway."

"I do."

And I did.

FREEDOM HIGHWAY

In 1972 I decided to leave Alex and the East Coast for California. I needed a radical change and felt the spirit leading me on. That spirit was expressed in music.

During my last weeks in New York, I spent hours walking through the poor sections of East Harlem and the white-glove territory of Park Avenue. On my portable radio I listened to Barbra Streisand, Roberta Flack, and Sarah Vaughan, voices that made my spirit soar. One day I was riding a bus across Central Park when I glanced at a newspaper and read the words "Mahalia Jackson, dead at 60." The words took my breath away. Mahalia's great spirit had washed over me as a child. I adored the grandeur of her talent. Through Alex and others, I had met her in Chicago a number of times. She was especially kind and loving to the gay men in the community. She accepted us without judgment and counted us among her closest associates and friends. Her death was devastating.

Before I hopped the Greyhound for Los Angeles, I bought a cassette tape, a new release, of the Staple Singers' *Freedom Highway*. I took that trip with Pops Staples and his children—Pervis, Yvonne, Cleotha, and Mavis—singing into my ear. I was transported, not merely by their heavenly family harmony but by their message. Vinnette had artfully married gospel and musical theater; now the Staples were using gospel to reach the masses with songs of social relevance. Their anthems—"Why (Am I Treated So Bad)?" "For What It's Worth," "Move Along Train," "Hammer and Nails," "Freedom Highway"—told me I had the right to take my singing talent wherever the spirit might lead. Pops's muddy Mississippi guitar was as funky as ever; Sister Mavis was moaning low; the glory of God was still being expressed; throughout it all, their theme was freedom, freedom to take your story wherever the spirit leads.

On that cross-country bus ride, I also carried a cassette of *What's Going On*. Before this breakthrough album, Marvin Gaye's previous hit had been "The End of Our Road." But, like the Staples, Marvin was interested in freedom—artistic freedom—and was tapping into his gospel roots to preach a new kind of sermon. He questioned the Vietnam War and bemoaned the damage done to our ecology. He protested police brutality in "Inner City Blues," drawing our attention to the disenfranchised. At the same time, he was proclaiming the essential Christian ethos that insists "God Is Love." The very thing that Marvin was reaching for—he called it "Wholy Holy," a union between the secular and sacred—was the Promised Land. The Freedom Highway I was on was leading me there, away from the confusion of the past into possibilities of right now. It was good; it was God; it was faith in the future and faith in the ever-changing flow of the events shaping my story.

The bus wound its way through the hills of Kentucky, into Missouri and the flatlands of Kansas, over the Colorado Rockies, through Utah and the Nevada desert and into California. When we arrived in Los Angeles, my head was filled with the encouragement I had found in the Staples and Marvin Gaye. I got off the bus expecting the best.

I call the decade between 1972 and 1982 my wilderness years. I was wondering and wandering. For the most part, I lived alone with my conscience. I came across temptations that sometimes got the better of me. Other times, I resisted and remained firm in my resolve to grow closer to God. I began this journey in dire poverty.

When I arrived in L.A., I went looking for Dionne and Dee Dee Warwick along with Estelle Brown and the Sweet Inspirations. They had all moved out to California some years before, and I knew they'd be glad to see me. I had an address for Estelle, who was renting a big house where she lived with Reverend William Morris O'Neill, who had also moved to L.A. Estelle loved Reverend—we all did—and, with her good salary from the Sweet Inspirations, helped support him. When I found the house, on Bronson off Wilshire Boulevard, it looked like a mansion. I rang the doorbell. A cute guy answered. I asked for Reverend.

"Wait here," said the cutie.

Of course Reverend recognized me immediately.

"Carl," he said, "what brings you to L.A.?"

"I quit Alex and figured I'd start over out here. Is Estelle home?"

"She's in Vegas with the Sweets. They're singing with Elvis at one of the big hotels."

"Well," I said, "I was figuring on staying with her."

"I'd have to ask her about that," Reverend said.

As soon as Reverend got Estelle on the line, she said, "Carl's my brother. He can stay as long as he wants."

I stayed, but only for a couple of nights. I didn't want to wear out my welcome. Reverend O'Neill was a good man, yet I had invaded his space, and I wasn't feeling comfortable about it. So I rode the bus downtown and walked the streets with my little Panasonic cassette player pressed to my ear with the Staples family singing "I'll Take You There." The farther I walked and the more homeless people I saw, the more I worried about finding work. I checked into a cheap hotel, but after a few days of job hunting, I was still unemployed and flat broke. I went to

Travelers Aid, where they directed me to the Unattached Men's Center, a mission below Main Street. It was a welfare program run by the city. When I arrived, I saw that it was set up for people just out of prison or down on their luck.

"Sometimes we'll find you work ourselves," said the man at the mission. "On those days when we don't, we'll give you some silver money and vouchers for a hotel and meals. One way or the other, we'll help you get through."

When I think back, it's strange that, with the Equity card that I had gotten in New York through Vinnette, I didn't seek work in the theater. After all, Hollywood was only a few miles from Downtown. Didn't I belong in Hollywood? But something stopped me from pursuing that path. Something kept me on the streets with the hapless and homeless. I had never been on welfare. I didn't know that world. But I was amazed to discover that my desperation was as real as that of the man looking for handouts. At the same time, a certain calmness reassured me that I needed to be among the disenfranchised. The Holy Spirit was pushing me on.

The first night I stayed at the dorm in the mission, a long room lined with cots. It wasn't pleasant, but it was better than the streets. Before going to sleep, I took my little suitcase, cassette player, and other belongings, and put them under the bed.

"Better not do that, son," said a man in the cot next to mine. "Better put all your things in the bed with you. Keep your arms around them or they won't be there in the morning."

He spoke with such kindness that I stopped to look in his eyes. He sensed my vulnerability and said, "Is this your first time at a place like this?"

"Yes."

"Well, nothing to be ashamed of. God loves us in all our conditions. He loves us when we're down just as much as when we're up. You know that, don't you?"

"I know it," I said, "but it's good to be reminded."

"I need to remind myself that his grace ain't conditional on anything. It just is. He can't do nothing but love us. That's just who he is."

"That's how it was taught to me," I said.

"Well, they taught you well, son. Now go to sleep. Glad to have a chance to share this little moment."

That little moment meant a lot. In the loneliness of a mission for the down-and-out, it reconfirmed my faith that God hadn't abandoned me and never would. God showed up in the form of that stranger, whom I would never see again. God spoke through him and said, "You're not alone." That same night I had the first of a series of prophetic dreams. As time went on, they became more detailed. They became so astounding that I even began to keep a journal. In these dreams, men were crying. Men were dying. Men were bandaged and reaching out for help. There was despair and deep depression. The air was thick with disease. When I awoke, I felt shaken to the core. I didn't understand why I was dreaming what I was dreaming. I didn't understand anything.

Next day I was told by the Unattached Men's Center to report for work at the County General Hospital, a sprawling facility that a few years later would be the setting for the most dramatic chapter of my life. For now, though, my job was to sweep the parking lot. I was happy to do just that, put in a full day's work, and earn the minimum wage.

Homeless men began to tell me their stories. Some were drunks, others junkies. Some bore the wounds of mental illness. Others had physical afflictions—blindness in one eye, a collapsed lung, cancer of the stomach or the liver. They needed to talk. They needed to explain how they had arrived at this point. Some had begun with money and had lost it all. Others had started out poor and gotten even poorer. Wives had been lost, children had been abandoned, good careers had turned bad. Every circumstance was different. Every story had its own peculiar shape. And so I listened. At the beginning, I didn't think I was capable of such intense listening. Late at night or early in the morning, in the dorm of the mission or the coffee shop across the street, I thought I'd have to excuse myself. It wasn't my job to listen to them; I needed to find work so I could eat. But I stayed. I found a patience that I didn't recognize as my own. Something held me in place and kept me listening. Only later did I come to see that listening is a spiritual experience—that is, if you listen with your heart. My heart was broken by these stories, but I was encouraged when some of the men found the strength to move in a positive direction. One stopped drinking. Another stopped drugging. Still another found a job.

Sometimes I thought back to New York, where, rushing out of a Broadway theater, my friends and I would pass by a home-less man or woman on our way to Howard Johnson's for a late-night dinner. I might throw a dollar or two into their outstretched hands, but beyond that I gave them no thought. Their domain was not mine. I was a paid singer and performer. My friends were actors and poets. My mentor was a well-known director, a woman from the black bourgeoisie who had formed her own theater company and hobnobbed with intellectuals at the New School. I had a name in the gospel world. I was talked about as an up-and-coming star. I didn't look down on the vagrants who populated Times Square; I just didn't pay them any mind.

Now I was among them. I was no better or worse than they. I was beginning to recognize God's authorship in my life. He was unfolding a story through me, just as he does with everyone—that is, if we surrender our will to God. I was trying to do just that.

When I ventured out from the confines of Downtown, it was only to find work. While I swept the parking lots of County

Hospital, songs were starting to form in my head. I had to sing. I had to express the thoughts that had been haunting my heart. I wanted to reach people with those thoughts and celebrate the marriage of gospel and pop that the Staples had fashioned so successfully.

When I applied for office work at Prudential Insurance on Wilshire Boulevard, I told them that I was interested only in part-time work. I passed their tests with flying colors and was hired for half days. Lunch was free in their cafeteria.

Downtown, I often attended the Church of the Open Door. Next to it was a hotel where a black woman ran the kitchen and gave me my dinners for free. It was as though she and I had known each other our entire lives; she treated me like a son. On the weekends, I went to Pershing Square, an open park in the heart of Downtown that drew all sorts of people, where I would sit on a concrete bench and write. When I say "write," I don't mean with paper or pen. Melodies would float into my head. Lyrics danced through my imagination. Some vanished, but others returned. I saw titles written on the wind:

"Gotta Be Some Change Now."

"Something from Nothing."

"Redeemed."

"How the Fire Burns."

I also began hearing harmonies. I knew that I didn't want to sing these songs alone. I wanted a group. I wanted my own version of the Bradford Singers or the Staple Singers. I made the rounds of the black churches in L.A. known for their gospel music and recruited a few singers. Romeo sang bottom and Craig sang countertenor. Alvin, a fellow Baltimorean and former lover of my friend Ralph, was a superb pianist who had played with the Dorothy Norwood Singers. Royal, the heterosexual among us, became our drummer.

I loved the group, not only for their musical excellence but for their willingness to allow me to shape our sound. Everyone was eager to succeed. The path to success is rarely smooth. And ours was covered with land mines that blew our plans to smithereens when we weren't looking.

I stepped on one soon after the group started working together. One day, in the public men's room in Pershing Square, I walked in and noticed a man standing by the sink holding his crotch. That seemed an invitation, but I did nothing about it and instead walked to the urinal. Another man stood next to me. He was extremely attractive. He wasn't urinating, just standing there with an exposed erection. This excited me, but I was afraid to touch him. Instead I masturbated, ejaculated, and left. I didn't get more than a block away when the two men stopped me dead in my tracks.

"You're under arrest," they said.

"What for?" I asked.

"Indecent exposure."

"But you were the one exposing yourself," I told the guy who had stood next to me.

"Shut up and get in the car."

I was handcuffed and driven to jail. I didn't have enough money for my own attorney but knew enough to contact the American Civil Liberties Union. They sent over a Jewish lawyer who had a gay son and a reputation for helping same-sex-attracted people out of legal jams. When he heard my story, he said, "Carl, this is a clear case of entrapment."

"How will I convince the judge of that?"

"Just tell the truth. You speak well. You're obviously a man of character. Tell the judge everything that happened, including the fact that you masturbated. Don't try and sugarcoat anything. I'm counting on the judge recognizing an all-too-familiar pattern of entrapment. If the undercover cops also tell the truth, I think you'll walk out of the courthouse a free man."

The lawyer was right. I told the judge the unadorned truth and, much to my surprise, so did the policemen. The first admitted that he was holding his crotch; the second confirmed that he had exposed his erection.

"You have no record," the judge told me. "You've led a stellar life. This is a clear case of entrapment. I'm releasing you on your own recognizance. Case dismissed."

"We can help other people with this decision," the lawyer told me. "I can make you the Rosa Parks of gay entrapment. I want to publicize this case. I want to take it to the media."

My doubts got the better of me. I thought of my new group and the songs I wanted to sing. I wanted a career. I knew that making myself the poster boy for entrapment would hold up my plans. I declined.

Meanwhile, the Gay and Lesbian Center had just opened their offices on Wilshire near Union. It was just a couple of empty houses where gay people congregated and told stories about being harassed, persecuted, and belittled, often by members of their own family. I felt the beauty of having such a community and spent much time there. My world was rapidly changing, and even greater changes were just around the corner.

THE INDUSTRY

In the early seventies I founded a group called Carl Bean and Universal Love. For the first time, I began writing songs, both music and lyrics. I found a guy who had a little demo setup a few blocks away from Ray Charles's headquarters on Washington Boulevard just west of Downtown. For a couple of hundred dollars we cut two tunes—"Inflation," a song with echoes of the Pointer Sisters, and "How the Fire Burns," in the Harold Melvin and the Blue Notes/Teddy Pendergrass mode. I was pleased with the demos and wanted to get them out to the industry. But how? All I knew was to send my cassettes to the record companies. I got the names and addresses out of the phone book, put my little packages together with a cover letter, and was off to the post office.

Then I went on a fast, not as a way to petition God for a record deal but simply to clear my mind. I was always inspired by the scriptural references to fasting as a way to center myself within. It caused me to examine heart, motives, and behavior. I went without food or water, seeking guidance from the Holy Spirit.

Then my dreams returned.

More bandages.

More crying souls.

More people moving through hospitals.

More wailing.

More darkness.

In one dream I was in a room with a powerful preacher. I wanted to ask him the meaning of what I was seeing, hearing, and feeling. Who are these people? Why these bandages? Why this pain?

"Don't ask these questions," said the voice of God. "Don't ask this preacher. Don't ask your friends. Just follow me."

"To where?" I had to know.

"Keep fasting," was the answer. "Keep praying. Keep meditating. Keep your eyes open. See everything that's happening around you."

The voice stopped, the dream ended, and I awoke.

At the end of the fast, I ate my first meal in days and returned to the welfare hotel where I was staying.

"There's a message for you," said the switchboard operator. "Call Lee Young Senior at ABC Records."

I rushed to the pay phone.

"Mr. Young, this is Carl Bean."

"Hello there, Carl." His voice was friendly and filled with enthusiasm. "I have your tape. I like it very much. I'd like to meet you in my office. Is tomorrow too soon?"

"Not soon enough, Mr. Young. Whatever time you say, I'll be a half hour early."

Like Reverend Marcus Garvey Wood and Vinnette Justine Carroll, Lee Young Sr. became a guiding light in my life. He was a man of great erudition and dignity. He was the brother of perhaps the greatest of all saxophonists, the immortal Lester Young. Lee was also a drummer for Nat King Cole and had appeared with Nat in the film version of the life of W. C. Handy.

I thank God for my connection to Lee. I often wonder at the good fortune of meeting a guy of such integrity in an industry overpopulated with hustlers. Given my naïveté, I could have easily been swindled, but Lee took on the role of a mentor and a teacher. I started calling him "Pop."

"This material you've produced shows me a great deal," he said. "I like the songs, I like your voice, and I like the production. I presume you were the producer."

"I was."

"Well, Carl, you have a big talent. And I want to sign you to ABC. But while you're assembling your materials and getting ready for the studio, I want you to do a little studying."

"What kind of studying, sir?"

"I want you to get in touch with our musical roots."

I wasn't sure what he meant. I knew gospel and I thought I knew rhythm and blues. I told Lee I'd been singing and hearing that kind of music since I was a kid.

"I'm talking about the kind of music being played before you were born—the roots of rhythm and blues."

Next thing I knew I had my own personal tutor. Lee played me record after record by Big Joe Turner, Big Mama Thornton, Eddie "Cleanhead" Vinson, Amos Milburn, and Roy Brown, artists who dominated the black music charts in the late forties and early fifties. They had big voices and tremendous charisma.

"You have that same kind of charisma," said Lee.

From his mammoth record collection, he pulled out albums by the original masters—Ma Rainey, Mamie Smith, and Bessie Smith. Their sound knocked me out. I could hear how Bessie was to blues what Mahalia was to gospel—a force of nature that had changed the musical weather for decades to come.

"You also need to read about the music," said Lee.

He gave me books—*Honkers and Shouters* by Arnold Shaw and *Blues People* by LeRoi Jones. I learned how we had invented a form that miraculously transformed misery to joy, a music that became a strategy for physical, financial, and spiritual survival. Reading this history, I felt part of something far bigger than myself.

"If you go into show business," Lee explained, "it's the

business part you can't neglect. The money, Carl, is in the publishing rights. You must control your own copyrights to your own songs. Don't give these copyrights away. Fats Waller, one of our most gifted writers, gave up all his copyrights for virtually nothing. Don't let that happen to you."

Lee not only gave me solid business advice but urged me to produce artists beyond my own group. I came to ABC in the early seventies when the label was in an especially aggressive acquisition/production mode. They had bought the Duke R & B and Peacock gospel labels from Don Robey in Houston. A decade before Berry Gordy began Motown, Robey was the most important black musical entrepreneur in America. He had not only record labels but a major publishing firm and booking agency. Bobby "Blue" Bland, Johnny Ace, and O. V. Wright were all Duke artists, and the Peacock roster included the Five Blind Boys of Mississippi, the Sensational Nightingales, the O'Neal Twins, the Mighty Clouds of Joy, and the Dixie Hummingbirds.

"I want you to go to Philly and produce the Hummingbirds," Lee said to me. "No reason they can't hit as big as the Clouds, who were on *Soul Train* last week. Imagine—a gospel group on *Soul Train*! Look, Carl, you knew what to do with your own group, and you'll know what to do with the Birds. There's also a gospel singer named Liz Dargan. I want you to produce her."

The City of Brotherly Love was, of course, the home of Gamble and Huff, whose Philly International label had created, after Motown, the new sound of black music. Along with Harold Melvin, they cut hits on the O'Jays, LaBelle, Billy Paul, Lou Rawls, the Jones Girls, and the Jacksons. Lee had set me up in a Philly studio, where he was convinced I'd produce a slew of masterpieces. Instead of plunging headfirst into the project, though, I panicked. I couldn't read or write music. I didn't play any instruments. And though I had recorded with Alex and others, I had never supervised a big-time session. The demos I produced for

Universal Love I'd made in a small local studio. Philly was something else. I loved the Birds—and especially their lead singer Ira Tucker, a gospel immortal—and I knew the voice of Liz Dargan, my homegirl, who sang like gospel diva Ruth Davis. Liz was great, Ira was great, and Lee was great for believing in me, but in 1973 I lacked belief in myself. Just before I was due to leave for Philadelphia, I bailed.

You'd think Lee would have been angry. After all, he'd gone out on a limb. But my sage mentor was always understanding.

"If you're not ready to produce others, you're not ready," he said. "Let's just hope your own album makes some noise."

Carl Bean and Universal Love: All We Need Is Love came out on ABC/Peacock, the gospel subsidiary. I argued against that. I thought we had pop hits and asked Lee to put me in the same ABC R & B/pop stable with the recently signed Rufus and Chaka Khan.

"Can't do that, Carl," he said. "That's a separate division, just like the blues division, with Bobby Bland and B. B. King. It operates autonomously. You were signed as a gospel artist. You can, however, pick out your single."

I chose "Gotta Be Some Change" as our first single because Romeo sang lead and not me. I was determined not to be overbearing like other group leaders, who couldn't tolerate anyone else having a hit. I wanted to make sure that the guys in my group got their turn in the spotlight. But neither "Gotta Be Some Change" nor "Something for Nothing," our second single, hit the charts. The ABC execs complained that our sound fell in the cracks between gospel and pop—too gospel for the pop stations, too pop for the gospel deejays.

The truth is that we were ahead of the curve. I was part of a movement looking to erase the line between R & B and gospel. The Staples had certainly contributed to the melding of the two genres, but the acceptance of a truly integrated gospel/pop sound was still years away. Today, for example, Kirk Franklin sounds as R & B as R. Kelly, and R. Kelly employs musical motifs right out of gospel. Back then, there was skepticism, from both the record company and deejays, when a gospel group sounded too secular. Consequently, we were viewed as neither here nor there.

There weren't enough sales to justify a national tour, but Pop made sure the group performed live. "Rather than have you go out with gospel groups," he said, "let's experiment. Let's put you in underground clubs, the venues where progressive white rock is played. I have a hunch they'll love you there."

They did. They also loved blues singers like the great Joe Turner, whom I had the privilege to meet up close and personal at one such club. He was a mountain of a man who, in his twilight years, sang while seated in a chair. He told me stories of the old days and expressed gratitude for his ability to still sing forcefully. From seminal artists like Joe, rock and roll vocalists learned to sing forcefully. Their fans expect as much. So when I got up there and gave it all I had, the response was tremendous. Standing ovations in every club. And yet little airplay. Through it all, though, Universal Love held together. By luck, I had found an inexpensive rental house with room enough for everyone. As with all groups, though, there were problems. The fact that our record wasn't selling was difficult enough. Money was tight. A few of the guys were heavy into weed, wine, and other substances. I tried to discipline them, but it didn't work. Eventually, I had to let the group go. Meanwhile, the dreams returned. The cries for help. The bandages. The hallways in hospitals. Doctors. Death certificates. Why? What did it all mean? What did these dreams mean?

WOUNDS

One hot Friday in late June, I spent all day writing my dreams in a journal. My small apartment was stifling. I had no air conditioning, and my little electric fan did little good. It was cooler outside than in, so I decided to go out for a walk. Sixth Street had the feeling of an older L.A.—the thirties or forties. I liked being thrown back in time. I used my afternoon to commune with God in nature. I went over the circumstances of my life—the day that Mrs. Wood knocked on my door in Baltimore and recruited me into her brother-in-law's socially progressive church; the way Dr. Freund ministered to my spirit; how I met Alex Bradford and the gospel music experience he afforded me; how Vinnette had expanded my culture and vision; how the Lord had made me understand the necessity of loving everybody. I was overwhelmed with feelings of gratitude.

I was leaving the park that surrounds the L.A. County Art Museum and the La Brea Tar Pits when a voice exploded out of a loudspeaker attached to a cop car: "*Stop right there!*"

I looked around. Surely that order couldn't be meant for me.

"Yes, you. Don't move!"

A policeman jumped out and pinned me against a wall.

"Hands up!"

"What . . . ," I started to protest.

"Shut up, nigger. Just shut up."

At that moment, another policeman got out of the back seat accompanied by an elderly woman who pointed at me and screamed, "That's him! He took my purse and nearly ripped off my arm!"

I wasn't allowed to protest. I was handcuffed and thrown in back of the squad car.

"When are you niggers going to stop mugging the old Jewish ladies around here?" asked one cop.

"That's what niggers do," answered the other.

At the station on Venice Boulevard I was ordered to line up against a wall. They took a mug shot and, out of nowhere, threw a purse at me.

"Catch!" one of the cops cried.

Instead, I ducked. I later realized that the only reason they couldn't press charges was that they needed my fingerprints on that purse—the one the woman claimed I'd stolen. Nonetheless, they threw me in the slammer for the weekend. Given one call, I phoned the only lawyer I knew, but he was unavailable.

"This is dead time," said the cop. "You're dead till Monday."

At first he was going to throw me in a cell where a brute of a man was screaming about what he intended to do with me. Fortunately, the cop took pity on me and found another cell with four bunk beds. Of my three cellmates, one was a Christian and a protector. "No one's gonna touch you, Rev," he said. To this day I still don't know why he used that designation.

It was a long weekend, but early Monday I was released. The captain said, "Your story checks out. Chances are you are not the perpetrator. Now get out."

No apology was offered.

"You're going to be okay, Rev," said my protector.

"I can't thank you enough," I said.

"It's a blessing, Rev. It's all a big blessing."

———

Another racial incident rattled me. I was invited to a gathering of friends on a Saturday night. It was a show business crowd. The evening was lively, the fellowship warm, and the food good. When I left to catch the bus home, I was feeling especially happy. It was a pleasant evening, so I decided to walk to the bus stop, some six blocks down La Brea Avenue. There I stood alone, waiting for the bus, when a car pulled up. Three men were seated inside.

"Excuse me," said one of them, "can you tell us the way to the Hollywood Bowl?"

"Of course," I said. As I began speaking, the man said he couldn't hear. Would I mind moving closer to the car? I was happy to accommodate him. With me standing less than a foot from the curb, he pulled a spray can, hit the button, and directed the spray into my eyes.

"Nigger!" he screamed. "We got your black ass!"

I fell to my knees. The pain was incredible. I was blinded. No one was around to help me. I didn't know what to do, so I finally made my way to the bench in front of the bus stop. I sat for a few minutes, trying to open my eyes, but each time I did, the burning was unbearable. I took a deep breath and gathered my wits. I remembered that a friend lived around the corner. Somehow, taking tiny halting steps, I stumbled over there. Thank God she was home. As soon as she saw me, she said, "Carl, you've been maced. Let me wash your eyes with water."

The water worked. I was okay. My eyes still burned for hours, but the more searing pain went to my heart. Within a few weeks, I had been assaulted twice—first by the police, now by these men. It's hard not to personalize racism. It's hard not to retreat to feelings of victimization. It's hard not to turn to rage. It's hard to forgive that kind of mean-spirited behavior. I do not claim to have found forgiveness immediately. I had been frightened. Fright led to anger. But, thank God, my training, especially in the early civil rights days in Baltimore, had addressed the issue of abuse. How do we react when we're brutalized by an aggressor? Our human desire, of course, is for revenge. We want to wound those who wound us. But I was taught to respond not with revenge but with love. It took a while to get to that love. But I somehow managed to pray for the cops who cursed me and the guys who maced me. Praying for them was the only way to lose my fury. Praying for them was the only way to reach God—and allow God's love to win.

ELLA FITZGERALD IS SHOPPING FOR LAMPS

I was selling lamps at the May Company at the corner of Wilshire Boulevard and Fairfax Avenue in the district called the Miracle Mile. And boy, at that moment in my life, did I ever need a miracle!

One afternoon, I was approached by the great Ella Fitzgerald. She spoke like we were old friends.

"I could sure use some help," she said.

"Yes, ma'am," I said. "I'd be honored, Miss Fitzgerald. I want to say that I've loved your singing my entire life. In fact, I *adore* your singing. I'm thrilled to be standing here next to you."

"I appreciate that, sweetheart, but here's what I need. I need some kind of little lamps that will light a room and make it feel like a speakeasy. Do you know what I mean?"

"I do."

"I knew you would. You see, Basie and the boys like to come over to my house in Beverly Hills. It's a big house but they don't like sitting in the living room or even in the den. They wind up hanging out in a little side room I have off the kitchen with a card table and a little record player. That's where they sit around smoking those cigars while they play poker and listen to old records. Problem is, the room is dark and those old cats need light."

"Well, I can solve that problem in no time, Miss Fitzgerald."

I showed her a couple of gooseneck lamps that would create the kind of mood she wanted.

"That's perfect," she said. "I'll take them both."

Before she left, I asked for her autograph. She gladly complied.

"You've warmed my day with kindness," she said. "And I'll be back to see you."

For whatever reason, Miss Fitzgerald liked to pay her May Company bill in person, and every month when she came in, she never failed to greet and encourage me. With my music career on hold, these little encounters meant the world to me.

On another afternoon when the tedium of selling merchandise was getting to me, I looked up to see Miss Gloria Lynne. Before I had a chance to tell her that I knew who she was, she began talking to me like an old friend. We chatted about incidental things, but soon the conversation turned serious. She had problems—deep personal problems—and, just like that, confided in me. I was touched.

"Miss Lynne," I told her, "I was once on the same flatbed truck with you in Harlem when I performed with the Gospel Wonders. I've also seen you at the Apollo many times. I was among those fans standing up and screaming when you started singing 'I Wish You Love.' We all loved you, and we still do. You're a wonderful artist."

From there, the conversation turned to the music profession. I explained the challenges I had faced. I told her about my New York church days, my time with Alex Bradford, Vinnette, and my own group on ABC. "I want to sing message songs like the Staples," I said, "but the record company is looking to pigeonhole me in a gospel category where I don't really belong."

"The record business is all about pigeonholing," said Miss Lynne, "but you stay true to your own individuality. You'll definitely make it, Carl, because your passion for the music couldn't be any more sincere, and sooner or later the people will hear that."

Encouragement never ceased. And neither did my dream of finding a romantic connection. It happened one night when a friend invited me over.

"Carl," said my friend, "meet Bret*. You and he have a great deal in common. You're both church boys."

Bret was ironing a shirt. He looked at me with dark, smiling eyes, offered his hand, and when our fingers touched, I felt that connection. A sweet and handsome guy, seven years my junior, he was visiting L.A. from Detroit. Bret had a story he needed to tell. He candidly explained that to please his own family he had married a woman. Their sex life was unsatisfying, and when he finally admitted his attraction to men, he and his wife divorced. He couldn't tell his family that he was gay, and rather than go on living a lie as a make-believe straight man in Detroit, he came to L.A.

"I was brought up in the holiness church," he said. "You know how Pentecostal preachers preach against homosexuals. If you're gay, you're doomed to hell. I'd hear those sermons and die inside. I'd fight my own feelings and tell myself I could free myself of those sinful desires. I didn't want to be who I was. I wanted to be a good Christian as the church defined a good Christian. But other than these condemning messages, I loved the church. The church meant celebrating God through beautiful song. The church gave me joy. How could you not love the church?"

We kept on talking and discovered that our musical passions were similar. Bret loved gospel and rhythm and blues. Like me, he loved Eddie Levert and Teddy Pendergrass. He was crazy for the Philly International sounds of McFadden and Whitehead. We talked about our favorite singers for hours. We sparked, and soon we were dating. Next we were a couple in love. By then I was living in the Fairfax district not far from my job at the May

Company. Bret moved in. This surprised and delighted me. Looking back, I see that I was following the pattern set by my adoptive dad. He took care of Mom, just as I was wanting to take care of Bret. Dad paid the bills. Now I paid the bills. Dad put Mom in pretty dresses. I put Bret in pretty kaftans. He called me twice a day and brought me roses. For the first time in a romantic relationship, I was the head of a household, while Bret accepted the role of housekeeper. I was discovering the joys of domestic stability and the beauty of loving a person whose strong sense of family matched mine.

But when I went to sleep, the dreams returned. God was surely leading me, but I didn't know where.

Then, one day at work, the phone rang.

I WAS BORN THIS WAY

A colleague at the May Company said that the call was for me.

"I'm with a customer right now," I said. "Please just take a message."

"They're insistent, Carl. It's Motown Records saying they've been looking all over for you. They have a song they want you to record."

"Very funny," I said.

"I'm telling you the truth."

"It's some crazy friend of mine being cute. Tell Motown I'm not interested."

"If you insist."

I forgot about the joke until the next day when Motown called again. Once again I was with a customer, and once again I refused to be the butt of someone's joke. When the third call came, I stood my ground. I hung up in the caller's ear.

Then came a messenger with a large envelope in hand. He walked right up to me while I was dusting lampshades and said, "Are you Carl Bean?"

"Yes."

"This is for you."

The return address carried the famous Motown logo. Inside was a note from Gwen Gordy, the sister of Berry Gordy. She was an executive at the company and she had a song she wanted me to sing. Attached were lyrics for what would be the first openly gay anthem recorded in disco, the red-hot sound that had been sweeping the country. All this information amazed me. When I read the lyrics, I was even more amazed.

The song was "I Was Born This Way," with lyrics by Bunny Jones, a straight woman from New York, and music by Chris Spierer. Ms. Jones had owned beauty salons in Harlem, had many gay friends, and felt moved to write something that expressed the pride in their hearts. She also wanted to raise their spirits. The lyrics said, "I'm walking through life in nature's disguise. You laugh at me, you criticize. Because I'm happy, carefree, and gay. 'Tain't a fault, 'tis a fact. I was born this way."

I couldn't quite believe it. It was as though the writer had read my very own heart. I went to the phone and called Ms. Gordy.

"I'm so glad I reached you, Carl," she said. "Come over right away."

I ran.

Motown had moved from Detroit to Los Angeles some eight years earlier. The first decade of Motown—the sixties—had redefined the very nature of black music, giving it wider popularity. That was owing to both the brilliant singers (Smokey Robinson, Little Stevie Wonder, Martha Reeves, Mary Wilson, Marvin Gaye, the Supremes, the Four Tops, and the Temptations) and the amazing stable of master writer/producers (Holland-Dozier-Holland, Harvey Fuqua, Johnny Bristol, Ashford and Simpson, Norman Whitfield, and Smokey Robinson). I loved Motown. Everyone did.

At the end of the sixties, Gordy concentrated on two primary acts—the Jackson Five, who had exploded with hit after hit, and Diana Ross, who had quit the Supremes to go solo. Berry turned Diana into a movie star in *Lady Sings the Blues* and *Mahogany* while establishing himself as a Hollywood mogul. His new headquarters were in a high-rise building on Sunset Boulevard.

Instead of inviting me to the building, Gwen Gordy invited me to her home in Beverly Hills. I was struck by the life-size oil painting of her brother Berry dressed as Napoleon. Gwen was a brilliant no-nonsense business lady. Before we started talking about my situation, she introduced me to her recently signed group, High Inergy.

"This is their first single," she said. "What do you think?"

The song was "You Can't Turn Me Off (in the Middle of Turning Me On)."

The beat was infectious and the lyrics were cute. "I think it's a hit," I said.

"I *know* it's a hit," she confirmed.

"How in the world did you know about me, Ms. Gordy?" I asked.

"Lee Young, Senior. He's been working over here, along with his son Lee Junior. One day Lee Senior was blasting that record you made when he was still working at ABC. Berry happened to be walking by Lee's office and heard it. 'Who in the hell is that?' he asked. 'Carl Bean,' said Lee. 'This guy's something else, Berry. Listen to the whole record.' Berry loved what he heard. When he played it for me, I felt the same. That's when Berry told me about this special song. We initially put it out on the Motown subsidiary label Gaiee sung by a man called Valentino. But his version didn't work for the disco market. When Berry heard your voice, he said, 'Bean would be perfect. It's a message song with a gospel feel. Bean will tear it up.'"

We tossed around some production ideas before I asked if I could be directed to Pop's office. When I arrived, Pop looked up and smiled.

"Where have you been hiding, Carl?" he asked. "When you wouldn't even take our calls, I figured you had gone off the deep end."

"The Lord wouldn't let me do that, Pop."

"I don't know about the Lord, but *I* wouldn't let you do that. Not when Berry found this hit for you."

"I Was Born This Way" was definitely disco, the dance craze of the seventies. It was similar in spirit to the swing music that hit in the forties, the R & B and rock and roll that dominated the fifties, and the Motown/Stax soul music that defined the sixties, but it had distinct qualities that were profound on many levels. Unlike rock and roll, disco required dancing skills. Think of Travolta in *Saturday Night Fever*, the ultimate disco movie. In the words of Barry White, whose busy bass lines and swirling strings established many of disco's musical motifs, disco was "a beautiful music for beautiful people not afraid to dress beautifully." Rock and roll was wear-what-you-want. Disco was dress-up-to-the-nines, high energy, high steppin' on the dance floor. More importantly, disco came out of a culture that was largely black and gay. It reflected two of the decade's great social movements—women's liberation and black liberation. The majority of disco singers were black and female, and gay men were its first and most loyal fans. Disco had gay written all over it.

The best of disco music was inspiring. Gloria Gaynor's disco-ized version of "Never Can Say Goodbye" and her glorious "I Will Survive" are undisputed masterpieces. The same is true of Donna Summer's "Last Dance," "MacArthur Park," "Hot Stuff," "Bad Girls," and "On the Radio." Marvin Gaye's nod to disco— "Got to Give It Up," an autobiographical song about a man conquering his fear of dancing—is a gem. I was taken with the disco hit of former gospel star Candi Staton, "Young Hearts Run Free," as well as Evelyn "Champagne" King's haunting "Shame." I adored the restrained elegance of Chic's "Dance, Dance, Dance (Yowsah, Yowsah, Yowsah)," "Le Freak," and "Good Times." And of course Sylvester, a magnificent singer who found the courage to perform in drag, crafted artful records, including "Dance (Disco Heat)," "You Make Me Feel (Mighty Real)," and "I (Who Have Nothing)." While still with his brothers, Michael Jackson sang a scorching lead vocal on "Dancing Machine," "Blame It on the Boogie," and "Shake Your Body (Down to the Ground)," each an example of high-quality, high-energy disco. "The Hustle," written and recorded by the great Van McCoy, lives on as perhaps the era's great instrumental.

Yes, sir, I could get with disco.

Meanwhile, Bret and I had broken up. Still unsure about his sexuality, he had moved back to Detroit. I loved him—I still do—but couldn't give him what he wanted. Simple domestic happiness in a committed relationship—like that of my cousin Carroll and his partner Andrew or my gospel colleague Charles and his spouse Smitty—seemed always just beyond my grasp.

Things started moving quickly with my Motown deal. The production of the song was given over to Norman Harris, Ron "Have Mercy" Kersey, and T. G. Conway. Norman was a guitarist and founding member of MFSB (Mother Father Sister Brother), the sensational stable of musicians that created the Philly International Sound along with producers Kenny Gamble, Leon Huff, and Thom Bell. Kersey, who was in the Salsoul Orchestra with Norman, was also a member of the Trammps. He had cowritten their hit "Disco Inferno," featured in *Saturday Night Fever*. I couldn't have asked for a hotter production team.

Berry Gordy wanted my lead vocal produced in Los Angeles, not Philly, where the instrumental track was made. Ron Kersey flew in to supervise. When it came to selecting background singers, I called for my girls, the Sweet Inspirations. I contacted my forever friend Estelle Brown, and the next thing I knew, she and Myrna Smith were down at Mo-West Studios in the heart of Hollywood. The recording session happened in a blaze of light. The girls were brilliant, and I sang with every bit of strength and sincerity at my command. Ron was a wonderful producer. He gave us the freedom to take the song to church. We also realized that we needed to do it gospel style, which meant no overdubs—me and the girls singing live to each other. Many producers don't know how to record a big, booming, earthy voice. They tend to rein it in. Ron let me shout it out. He felt the power of the moment and let that power prevail. It was Holy Ghost power, prompting me, pushing me on. Here is what I sang that day.

> *I'm walking through life in nature's disguise—yeah*
> *You laugh at me and you criticize—yeah*
> *'Cause I'm happy, carefree and gay . . .*
> *Ain't no fault—it's a fact*
> *I was born this way*

Berry Gordy heard the song and said, "You've caught lightning in a bottle. Let's mix it and get it on the radio."

Tom Moulton did a sizzling mix and, in a blink of an eye, "I Was Born This Way" was racing up the charts. I had a hit. Gay people had a hit. But so did straight folks, who loved it as much as gays. The song became an anthem of liberation for everyone.

When Motown gave me my deal, I tried my best to get them to include Universal Love. But the Gordys said that it was my voice they wanted, not my group, so I had no choice but to go solo. When it came time, though, for my first promo event at a club for "I Was Born This Way," I insisted that Universal Love join me. I also insisted that the first live performance of the song be done at a disco in the black community. That club was Jewel's Catch One, located on Pico just off Crenshaw Boulevard in mid-city L.A. This wasn't West Hollywood or Beverly Hills; this was a hot spot frequented by black gay men. Because the music and dancing were cutting-edge, the club was also frequented by pop stars like Madonna, artists looking to learn the latest trends.

The night I came to Catch One, anticipation was high. Word had spread about a new gay artist. As far as my own appearance, many expected another Sylvester—a man in drag. Sylvester also sang with female feeling. Maybe the crowd was expecting the same from me. Whatever they were expecting, I think they were surprised to see me in a leather bomber jacket and a Donny Hathaway–style cap. It was a masculine look and, for disco, I sang with an especially masculine sound. I was dressed in my normal street attire and people recognized that style's authenticity. I wasn't interested in being a gay stereotype; I was confident enough to present myself as an everyday guy.

From the first lyrics, sung a capella—"I'm happy, I'm carefree, and I'm gay . . . I was born this way"—to the first *thump-thump-thump* of that dazzling four-on-the-floor disco beat, the crowd went crazy. They were shouting and screaming and jumping for joy. They made me come back and sing that dang thing five more times. They liked my masculine look, they liked my masculine voice, and they liked the message I was preaching. No doubt about it, we had church up in there. An hour later, when the commotion started to die down, the Motown promo man leaned over and whispered in my ear, "That's not a song, Carl. That's a legend."

My next appearance was at Studio One, the upper-crust disco on Santa Monica Boulevard in Boys' Town that catered to white gay men. Studio One was Los Angeles's answer to New York's Studio 54. In addition to a huge disco floor, the compound included a smaller club called the Backlot Showroom that featured divas like Bernadette Peters, Eartha Kitt, Barbara Cook, Chita Rivera, Sally Kellerman, and Liza Minnelli.

I had heard about some racial incidents at Studio One where black men were harassed, so on the night of my appearance, I arrived with a large contingent of black friends. While I went through the artist's entrance, they went to the front door. Just before I was set to sing, I got word that my friends had been denied entrance because they each didn't have two picture IDs. When I went on stage, I let management have it.

I announced to the audience, "Tonight I'm singing about being happy, carefree, and gay. Well, I'm sure enough gay, but I can't say that I'm happy and carefree to sing in a club with racist policies. When my friends—my black gay friends—went to the door tonight to get in, they were turned away because they didn't have *two* IDs. *Two IDs? Who's ever heard of asking for two IDs?* Were any of you guys asked for two IDs before getting in here tonight?"

A big roar of *"No!"* went up from the crowd.

"That's just what I thought. So before I start singing about being happy, carefree, and gay, I want to make sure that *all* my happy, carefree, and gay friends get to hear me sing, or else I ain't gonna sing at all."

"That's right, brother!" yelled one guy.

"Let 'em in!" yelled another.

"Let 'em *all* in!" the crowd began to shout in unison.

Before I knew it, my friends were admitted.

"That's what I'm talking about," I said, while the dance track started bubbling underneath me. "I'm talking about a time when discrimination—and I mean *all* discrimination— dies. Discrimination against gays. Discrimination against women. Discrimination against blacks. Discrimination against Latinos. Discrimination against *anyone*. I'm talking about a time when love erases the lines separating us, a time when we can be open about who we are and dance as sisters and brothers in a world that respects us for saying . . . I was born this way. Yes, Lord, I was born this way!"

With that, the disco exploded.

"The legend's getting bigger," the Motown promo man told me when I came offstage. "The legend's getting out of hand."

In the early months of the song's release, I was invited back to Studio One time and again. Now my friends were always welcome, even in the VIP room, where we met Thelma Houston, Loleatta Holloway, and Shirley Bassey. L.A.'s other important disco—the Circus on Santa Monica Boulevard—booked me for at least a dozen appearances. Next on tap was the big one—Studio 54 in New York—but just before we arrived, Motown pulled out.

"They're having tax problems, maybe even criminal problems," Gwen Gordy told me. "We're keeping our acts away from there until the smoke clears."

I was disappointed, but not for long. New York embraced the song with even more fervor than L.A. "I Was Born This Way" broke in New Jersey before reaching Manhattan. By the time I arrived in the tristate area, the deejays had it in superheavy rotation. There were lines around the block at every disco I played. I hit Newark, Patterson, Jersey City, Brooklyn, and Staten Island. I went to Chicago, Austin, and Baltimore, where I was treated like a conquering hero by my childhood friends. When I hit the big discos in San Francisco and Sausalito, the song was on everyone's lips. When I shouted out, "I'm happy, carefree, and gay," it turned into a massive sing-along. I loved the experience, not only because I was making good money for the first time in my life, but because I was spreading love with a message of hope.

Back in Los Angeles, I got word that Iris Gordy, Berry's niece, wanted to see me. A bright young woman, Iris told me that Motown was excited about my future and thought I had many more disco hits in me. She suggested that I work with Hal Davis, the veteran producer of the Jackson Five's smash hits "I'll Be There" and "Dancing Machine," and Thelma Houston's "Don't Leave Me This Way." Unfortunately, Hal and I didn't click. His recording sessions were more about partying than music. His manner was harsh and his supervision heavy-handed.

"I can't work with this man," I told Iris.

"I understand, Carl, but another opportunity has come up that's even more pressing. There's a new David Ruffin record that's ready to go, all except for the lead vocals. David's having personal problems. We've been patient with him, but his delays have gone on for a long time. Berry wants you to do the record."

"Me? Replace David Ruffin?"

David Ruffin was the original Temptation who sang "My Girl" and a slew of other timeless hits. As a solo artist, he recorded "Walk Away from Love," considered one of the great soul performances of all time.

"Yes, you," said Iris. "You have the power and emotional depth of David. This is a great opportunity. This record will take you from disco star to crossover star. It could make all the difference for your career, Carl. Let me play you the tracks and show you the lyric sheets."

The tracks were smoking-hot R & B. And the lyrics were all about love and sex—love and sex between a man and a woman. The man was calling to his woman, begging his woman, teasing his woman, pleasing his woman.

"I don't think I can sing these songs," I told Iris.

"Why not?"

"They're straight-up heterosexual."

"What's wrong with that?"

"I'm straight-up homosexual."

"I don't think that matters, Carl."

"I'm not so sure, Iris. After all, your publicity man, Bob Jones, has set up interview after interview where I've spoken as an openly gay man. His promotional materials have stressed the same thing. And those materials have gone out to the straight, gay, and black press. So for me to start singing love ballads to women makes no sense."

"Take a little time and think about it, Carl. I respect you greatly, and I love the spirit behind 'I Was Born This Way.' But I also hate to see you pass up the opportunity of a lifetime. With this group of songs, you could be the new Teddy Pendergrass. So please, just tell me you'll think about it."

"I'll do better than that, Iris. I'll pray on it."

THE PRAYERS, THE DREAMS

anyone. I was told that I must demonstrate a better way in Christ.

Another dream was about a girl:

She was young—maybe fourteen or fifteen—and abjectly poor. She struggled to feed her family. Walking home, she passed a man who was carrying a bag of oranges. When she asked for a few pieces of his fruit, he refused. She passed other men and women carrying bags of food. She begged for just enough to keep her parents and siblings from starving, but no one responded. No one even looked her in the eye. She walked by the fine homes of the wealthy, but their gates were closed, locked, and guarded by ferocious dogs. She kept walking until she could walk no longer. She saw a church and sought shelter inside. But the church doors were sealed. I somehow found myself in that church with her when I heard the voice of God say to me, "Give nourishment. Give her these oranges. Let her live."

In my journal I recorded this incident:

I was Christmas shopping in a department store when a gentleman struck up a conversation with me. We started talking about the spirit of Christ. He asked if I was a believer. "Yes, I am," I said. I told him a little of my story and how God was leading my life in a direction that I had never anticipated. Just then another man, who had overheard us, asked me, "Are you attending a church that believes every word of the Bible as the gospel truth? Do you go to a church where people speak in tongues? If not, God is *not* leading you and you're deceiving yourself. If you call yourself a Christian, there is only one way to worship Christ." The first gentleman protested. "I'm sorry," he told the fundamentalist, taking up my part, "but God has this good man exactly where he needs to be. God will get done through him exactly what needs to be accomplished." I was astonished by this gentleman's defense of me. There was a strength in his words and an incontrovertible conviction that

Dear Lord," I prayed, "not my will, but thy will be done. Guide me. Show me the way. I know you gave me this talent for singing. You gave me a strong voice. You made me in your image, as we're all made in your image. You gave me a heart to serve. But what form should that service take?"

After Iris Gordy offered me the David Ruffin tracks, my prayers went on for days. I prayed for clarity, I prayed for objectivity, I prayed that my ego—excited by the adulation I received when I sang on stage—not overwhelm my obedience.

And then the dreams resumed. They were so strong, so mysterious, and so unrelenting that I kept a journal. The minute I awoke, I wrote down everything I remembered:

I was surrounded by children. They were calling to me, but instead of saying "Carl," they were saying "Rev." "Help us, Rev. Pray for us, Rev. Please, Rev, keep us safe."

I had a dream about my childhood:

My adoptive parents were seated on either side of me. They kept pointing their forefingers in my face and saying, "Do this, do that. You did this wrong, you did that wrong." I grabbed both my ears and shook my head feverishly. I ran from their presence. I entered another space where I was given the words *Patience* and *Understanding*. I was told by a disembodied voice not to judge people. Not to bug people. Not to ridicule reinforced my own faith. It was a chance encounter that helped me enormously.

Two other powerful episodes brought me closer to God:

One evening, while taking a bath, I slipped into a meditative state. On the wall, written in blazing neon, I saw the word "inward." The word shined down like a light from heaven. Then came the words "God lives within each of us. God is life and all life is God. God gave you your life. You are his homosexual son."

The most powerful vision came early one morning while I was still in bed. I left my physical being. At first, I was frightened and fought against this out-of-body experience. After a few seconds, though, I let go. I floated over myself, when suddenly the wall of my bedroom opened onto the world. I saw oceans, forests, jungles, hills, and valleys. I saw life—animal life, human life, plant life—living in total harmony. I heard a voice say, "I am love and my love is for everyone."

One day while at the Motown offices to pick up a check, I met a young black man, no older than nineteen. I was standing in the lobby waiting for the elevator when I saw him waiting alongside me. Our eyes locked for a quick second. He pushed the button for the seventeenth floor. I got off at sixteen. Twenty minutes later, my check in hand, I was back in the lobby, about to head for the bank, when I noticed that same young man. He looked devastated, as if a doctor had just told him that he had terminal cancer.

"Is something wrong?" I asked.

A simple question from a genuinely concerned stranger opened up the floodgates. The guy's name was Bobby, and he had a burning need to talk. He told me that he was a former gospel singer determined to sing pop. "Me too," I said. "But everyone tells me I'll be betraying Jesus," Bobby added. "Everyone is wrong," I said. It was 3 P.M. and I asked if he'd eaten anything all day. He hadn't, so I invited him to a nearby restaurant, where we talked for hours. He told me about his life in Christ and his baptism in the Holy Spirit. He discussed his homosexuality and how it had led to further condemnation by his parents. They had disowned him and kicked him out of the house. He had based his vocal style on his idol, Michael Jackson, and was trying to get a deal, but so far no luck. "No one will sign a gay singer," Bobby said, "especially Motown." "Motown not only signed me, an openly gay man," I told him, "but gave me an openly gay song to sing." He was amazed. Down to his last dime and fighting a debilitating depression, he had no place to sleep, no place to go. As he spoke, tears streamed from his eyes. I told him he could stay at my place.

I knew that I could help this young man, and I invited him to my home. When we got there, he thought my invitation involved some sexual favor. I quickly told him that was not the case. That night he slept on the couch. When he woke up the next morning, I gave him a key to my place. "Son," I said, "you can stay here as long as you like."

Bobby stayed for six months. During that time, our relationship was chaste. I was his older brother, his uncle, and his dad. I was there to help him through his crisis. He was a beautiful singer. Bobby had remarkable technique, a wide range, and a sweet soul expressed in every song he sang. He felt certain that he was capable of securing a record deal. But the voices of his parents and the condemning church of his childhood kept telling him no. His guilt at not singing religious music was overwhelming. We spent night after night in thoughtful reflection and prayer. I told him much of my own story. I shared with him my profound conviction that it is not incompatible to embrace the truth of who you are and the love of God. "God is love," I kept stressing to Bobby. "God cannot do anything *but* love. His love for you is unconditional and without limits. Just love him as he loves you."

"Your words make a difference," he said. "Your words touch my heart."

Meanwhile, I had finally decided what to do about the Motown offer. I went to see Iris Gordy and said, "I want to thank you for thinking of me. Replacing David Ruffin would be a great honor."

"I'm glad you see it that way, Carl. We're ready to get you in the studio right now."

"I can't do it, though, Iris. I just can't."

"Why?"

"I came out as a gay artist. Everyone who bought, listened to, and danced to 'I Was Born This Way' realized that this was a statement of gay liberation. I made that statement. I must stand by that statement. Not to do so would be the height of hypocrisy. I'd be letting down the people whose souls I touched. If I started singing 'I love you, girl,' or 'I need you, girl,' or 'I want you, girl,' I'd feel like a fool. I wouldn't mean it. I also know that Berry Gordy would never let me change the lyrics to 'I love you, boy' or 'I need you, boy.'"

"You're right, Carl," said Iris. "Those lyrics can't be changed to reflect gay life."

"And I can't be changed either, Iris, so I'll just have to take a pass and wish you well."

By then it was the early eighties and the dreams had reached a new level of intensity; they were constant. Men were screaming my name, babies were dying, women wandered through deserted streets. I couldn't think about anything else.

Time passed, and about a year later newspapers began carrying stories about a disease that seemed to be primarily infecting gay men. Articles first described the illness as GRID— gay-related immune deficiency syndrome. The Gay Men's Health Crisis, among the first organizations to deal with the disease, pointed out the unfairness of that name. Gay people weren't the only ones infected. If you are HIV positive, it means that you have tested positive for human immunodeficiency virus, even if you have no symptoms. AIDS—acquired immune deficiency syndrome—is the disease caused by the virus. Whatever the terms, this was terrible news.

I compiled a notebook containing as much information as I could find. The more I learned about the nightmare that the gay world was experiencing, the more the dreams made sense. I realized that the dreams were calling me to respond—but how?

"WHAT CONSTITUTES A CALLING?"

Suddenly it all came together—my experiences as a civil rights activist in the Jackie Robinson Youth Council, the progressive theology I had heard preached by Reverend Wood in Baltimore, my work in the ministry of gospel and message music, my profound relationship with Jesus Christ as defender of the downtrodden and lord of unconditional love. I knew that I had to go out into the community and involve myself, as an openly gay man, in the AIDS crisis. I also knew that, in this mission, I had to put my spirituality out front.

I discussed this burning desire with my dear friend Estelle Brown, who, in addition to being a Sweet Inspiration, had been ordained by Reverend O'Neill's Christian Tabernacle Church. Estelle mentioned my spiritual journey to Reverend O'Neill, who told her that he'd like to speak with me.

"Carl," said Reverend O'Neill, "what you have to do is far beyond what even you know. You're an important messenger of God's holy word. When I met you back in New York, you were already a devout Christian with an extraordinary background. All those years you spent in the gospel music ministry were invaluable training. Now I feel that you'd benefit from a fully accredited ordination from our denomination. If you're willing to put in the time for intense study, prayer, and fasting, you can come before my board of clerics for an examination."

I welcomed the opportunity. I entered a long period of scriptural study and solitary prayer as I sought spiritual enlightenment. At Reverend Troy Perry's Metropolitan Community Church, I attended a sacred service, foreign to my own background, yet moving and deeply Christian. The congregation was largely white and gay. When it was time to take communion, I stepped forward. As I stood in the aisle waiting to receive the sacraments, a white brother came to stand beside me. Without any prompting, he gently took my hand. As we approached the altar, we both knew that we were stepping into a heightened spiritual experience. After that, I attended Reverend Perry's Wednesday night Bible studies and read his autobiography, *The Lord Is My Shepherd and He Knows I'm Gay*. Reverend Perry and I became close.

I was also inspired by James Cone's many books, including *A Black Theology of Liberation*. The author of *Jesus and the Disinherited*, Howard Thurman, who taught Martin Luther King Jr., was another major influence on me. Thurman stated that not everyone who finds God may find him through Jesus, but a true seeker of God will encounter Jesus along the journey. In his autobiography, *With Head and Heart*, he illuminates scripture with a generous heart, not a narrow mind.

My mind was expanded by reading Eastern thought. *Autobiography of a Yogi*, by Paramahansa Yogananda, had a profound impact on my thinking. His sincere and tenacious search for a guru filled me with inspiration. I went to the Self-Realization Fellowship, dedicated to carrying out the service-oriented work of Yogananda. In the serene gardens that the Fellowship maintained in Santa Monica, I sat and felt a wonderful stillness, clarity of thought, and lightness of spirit. I experienced a new sort of baptism in unconditional love.

I spent months in the Downtown public library reading about theology and mysticism from diverse points of view. When my eyes tired from the printed page, I took the Wilshire Boulevard bus all the way to the beach, where I sat on the sand and breathed in the ocean. I became one with the ocean, one with the sky, the birds overhead, the children building castles. These were among the most beautiful moments of my life.

In August 1982, I went before the ordination board of Reverend O'Neill's Christian Tabernacle Church and passed their rigorous examination.

"You've done beautifully," said Reverend, "and I want to say that it is a blessing to grant you this fully accredited ordination. Beyond that, though, the spirit has moved us to go even further. Those of us who serve on this board have been led to grant you a charter to begin a church of your own."

I was amazed because I had not petitioned or even discussed such a sanction with Reverend or his board members. It was pure spirit that made them understand how God was doing a work in me that required—and would benefit from—ordination. The name "Unity Fellowship" came to mind. I knew that the word *unity* contained the right feeling.

The board members agreed that it was a fine name. "It has dignity and meaning," they said. "May God bless the Unity Fellowship of Christ Church."

So I had a name, but no building, no money, and no members. I had Christ, though, and in Christ I had everything. I also had the motivation to touch souls, and I knew that there was no better place to start than in my own backyard. I announced my ministry by placing a notice in the *Los Angeles Sentinel*, a widely circulated black publication. I wrote that I was "an openly gay" clergyman interested in bringing the Christian gospel to the lives of those who felt disconnected from the mainstream. I described how progressive theology—or liberation theology—saw Jesus' abiding love as inclusive, as opposed to exclusive, and how Jesus' grace meant grace for everyone.

Some homosexual Christian friends thought it inappropriate for me to describe myself as openly gay in such a public forum. I disagreed vehemently. I argued that those of us who were both Christian and gay could no longer live under a system of hypocrisy—that is, attend a church that pretended our sexual orientation didn't exist or, even worse, attend a church where it was condemned. Under that system, we had suffered deeply. We needed to be out. We needed to be open.

"Carl," said those friends who disagreed, "you'll drive people away. You'll antagonize. You'll alienate. You'll do more harm than good."

"I have no choice," I said. "I have gone too far to come back. The old way was all about shame. Now it's all about truth."

"Our community's not ready for it," they warned.

"Our community is hungry for it," I countered. "Our community is literally dying for it."

The *Sentinel* not only accepted the announcement for publication but ran it on the page with other *religious* announcements. I saw God's hand in that placement. The response was not overwhelming, but a few calls came in. Meanwhile, I began a study/support group for gay men and women in my little apartment on Cochran Avenue in the Fairfax district. We met every Monday night. When I put out the word among friends and acquaintances that I wanted to form a study group, I expected one or two to show up. But from the very start, at least a dozen people knocked on my door. We were a motley crew, in all sizes and colors, from all economic backgrounds. The differences didn't matter. We came together to share heartaches and joy about leading a spiritual life while not denying—nor defying—the fact of our homosexuality. The stories were painful: the lesbian who lost her job when her employer learned she was dating a woman; the gay guy whose father, after discovering his son's sexuality, disowned him and condemned him to hell; the aging queen, going on seventy, with a lifetime of tales documenting discrimination at every turn. These were people who needed to be heard.

The more the group members turned to me for wisdom, the more I turned to Christ. And the more I did that, the more they started calling me "Rev." Many of our members had been raised Christians. They had left the church or, more accurately, been thrown out of the church. In black churches, gays, although tolerated as choir members or soloists, were subjected to at least three sermons a year—one about Sodom, another about Leviticus, and a third about Romans. Each sermon used speciously literal interpretations to bash homosexuality. No preacher could ever explain why Jesus never himself condemned, or even mentioned, same-sex attraction. No preacher could justify why he selected certain Old Testament passages forbidding certain practices while ignoring others—eating shellfish, for example, or wearing two different fabrics together.

Debating scripture is an inevitable practice that often sheds little light. The major point I made to my group was this: Jesus is all about *inclusion*, not exclusion. His simple but radical outlook as the rabbi of love was simply that love is available to all. He was a Jew, but his ministry went far beyond Jewish culture or religion. He hung out with outcasts. He nursed the sick, the blind, and the insane. He lived his life so that the divine within him excited and activated the divine within us. The notion that Jesus would exclude same-sex-attracted humans from his all-inclusive grace went against the very essence of his miraculously loving nature. I went to Romans 8 and quoted that powerful passage, "For I am sure that neither death nor life, nor angels nor rulers, nor things present nor things to come, nor powers, nor principalities, nor height nor depth, nor anything else in all creation, will be able to separate us from the love of God in Christ Jesus our Lord."

"This is a time," I said, "when we are being tested as

Christians. Are we willing to tell our stories? Are we willing to describe our journeys with Christ?

Meanwhile, in the world around me, fears about the virus grew in every quarter, including my own mind. I was as afraid as anyone. People with whom I had been sexual had the telltale symptoms. Many would soon die. Any time the smallest bruise appeared on my arm or neck, I panicked, convinced that it was Kaposi's sarcoma, the skin cancer associated with HIV/AIDS. I spent my nights in anguish and filled my days with thoughts of my own demise. I could not view this disaster as an objective outsider. I was part of the communities under assault—both the gay and the black communities. I also understood that when it came to AIDS, my commitment was to the vast human community.

Specifically in the black community, not a single treatment center existed. I knew of no black church willing to openly express solidarity with homosexuals. No black church was saying, "We love you. We will care for you. As Jesus tended to the lepers, we will tend to you. We will comfort you with the abiding love that Christ instilled in us. You are our children. This is your home. Come home to us."

My life, my dreams, my social commitment learned at Providence Baptist in Baltimore, my feeling for the Lord of love culminated at this moment and in this place. In spite of—or because of—my own fears about dying of this dreaded disease, I had to do something to help my people. While the community stayed silent, I simply couldn't. I had to act. I had to become unconditional love.

SHANTI

I read about a volunteer-based approach that was dealing with people with AIDS called Shanti. I didn't know what "Shanti" meant, so when I went to the group's office on Santa Monica Boulevard, it was the first thing I asked. Their director, a clinical social worker named Jerry Coash, greeted me warmly and said, "*Shanti* is a Sanskrit word meaning inner peace or tranquillity. Our purpose is to provide some degree of peace and comfort to people with life-threatening or chronic illnesses."

The Shanti volunteers had been taught the specific skills necessary to provide hospice care to patients in grave condition. To go with them to the clinics and hospitals, I'd need to learn those skills.

"How can I help?" I asked Jerry.

"You can answer our phones. They're ringing off the walls."

So I answered the phones. This simple task was a critical starting point. Those calls were my first contact with people with HIV/AIDS, and they were riveting, enlightening, and disturbing. People were desperate, overwhelmed by fear. They were afraid, as was I, that each little bruise meant imminent death. They had also been given false information about the disease—that it could be transmitted by touching or breathing the same air as someone with HIV/AIDS. For weeks, I did nothing but pick up the phone and listen to the intense anxiety coming from the other end of the line. When I left at night, that fear and uncertainty went home with me.

I learned that Shanti's mission was all about peer support. In simple terms, it's the buddy system. As their pamphlets stated, "Our techniques are a way of being with another person that frees both parties to be fully who they are and share their feelings. It is a way of being which allows two persons to meet as equals. It is a way of relating to others that is characterized by certain values and attitudes." The values underlying the Shanti model of peer support are mutual respect, positive regard, empowerment of the client, genuineness—being oneself, authenticity—acceptance of differences, empathy, and commitment to service.

The techniques were broken down into three categories: listening from the heart, speaking from the heart, and acting from the heart. Overriding everything was a principle that I recognized as Buddhist: presence. Shanti stressed being present above all. Being in the moment. In the now. Engaging the patient with one's whole being.

As a Christian, it didn't bother me that the spiritual basis of Shanti relied on Buddhism. In my mind, those precepts are not incompatible with the teaching of Christ. Jesus taught, lived, and loved in the now. I thought about that moment in the Old Testament when Moses asks God to identify himself. God's answer is "I am that I am." God exists only in the present tense, the now. Shanti adamantly believed that healing exists in the now. To heal another's heart requires presence of mind, spirit, and soul. I loved that teaching. It was all about giving. Like Jesus' life on earth, it was all about service. Shanti helped me understand Christ beyond the Jesus of Nazareth; more than a specific man who lived at a specific time, Christ radiated a power that was always present.

Over two weekends at West Hollywood Park, Jerry Coash conducted a course to give us volunteers the current level of

AIDS information from the medical community and reinforce the methods we had learned for treating clients. We gained enough knowledge to become a buddy, and were then assigned to someone with HIV/AIDS and became their primary support person for the next year.

"You're going to have to be prepared to take on some abuse," Jerry warned us. "You may well be the first person these patients can sound off to. These people have been abandoned and in many cases neglected, even by their own doctors and nurses. Almost all of them are frightened. Many are angry, even furious. Some will be difficult for you to look at. You will not want to touch them. You may not even want to go near them. But you will. You will touch them, you will hold them, you will share your love with them. Whatever questions they ask you, you will answer honestly and to the best of your ability. You won't give them bogus hope and unrealistic predictions about cures. You will comfort them with the mere fact of your presence. You will look at them attentively, give them strong eye contact, and stay as long as you need to stay. You may well be the most important human being in their lives. You may be the difference between fear and faith. By your staying the course, their spirit will be renewed, and so will yours."

The last segment of the training was the most profound. Jerry termed it a guided meditation. Each volunteer was asked to sit alone, close his eyes, and imagine that he was awaiting the results of his HIV test. We sat there for fifteen long minutes, thinking about the possibility of being told that we were positive. "Think about what's at stake," said Jerry. "Think about what you are about to hear." After that long silence, Jerry, playing the part of a doctor, read the results. We were positive. We had the virus. Nearly all of us, pretending to be clients, broke down in tears.

"If you can't feel—and I mean deeply feel—what's happening to these people," said Jerry, "you can't possibly help them."

Jerry showed great sensitivity when he said to me, "Carl, I know how you love your own people. And I know about the extraordinary verbal gifts of black people. The culture has produced so many great singers, preachers, and actors. You yourself are wonderfully verbal, Carl. But I must advise you that there are times when words are insufficient. Words may even hinder. There are times when it's enough just to sit and hold a hand. Silence, loving silence, can do wonders. I hope you don't take offense at these remarks."

"I love your remarks, Jerry," I said. "All this is new territory for me, and I need all the advice I can get."

After my training was over and I was prepared to see my first client, I went back to our Monday study group and told them what I had been doing.

"Christ not only called me to love," I said, "but also to action."

As the HIV/AIDS virus spread, these weekly meetings grew more intense. Everyone in our group knew of at least someone with symptoms. A friend of mine who danced with Alvin Ailey in New York was infected. Making matters worse, a vocal segment of the public used AIDS to fuel their condemnation of homosexuality. Many reactionary preachers, blacks as well as whites, called this health crisis a punitive plague sent down from God.

The group members said they too wanted to work with AIDS patients. That's when I created a new buddy model, based on Shanti, but geared toward African Americans. I knew that our people needed to hear specifically about Christ. The language surrounding Jesus rang with a truth and brought a comfort that no other could provide. I put my idea to Jerry Coash as plainly as possible.

"I love Shanti," I told him, "and I love the work you do. But I can no longer continue to do this work out of your office. I need to take what you've taught me and bring it south of Wilshire

Boulevard. I need to take it to my own people. I hope you understand."

"I more than understand you, Carl," he said, "I encourage you. We're getting calls all the time from hospitals like County and Martin Luther King where HIV/AIDS patients need help. We have no one to send down there, no one who's been trained as thoroughly as you."

"The training's been fabulous. I'd be lost without it, Jerry, but I realize that I have to tweak your training model. I need to redefine it under the name of Jesus, both because I am a follower of Jesus and because it's the name Jesus that has the mightiest spiritual resonance with my people. If I'm to give these patients a level of comfort, I need to tap into their heritage, their hearts, and the scriptures that will bring them peace."

"You do whatever you have to do," said Jerry. "The language doesn't matter. All that matters is the love behind the language."

THE REV RESPONDS

USA *Today* ran an article about the AIDS crisis entitled "Six Who Made a Difference." I was one of the six people featured, and the only black. My hope was that the publicity would bring attention to my mission. To some degree it did. The article, though, that helped the most appeared during the summer of 1985 in the *L.A. Times*, written by Lynn Simross: "The Rev. Responds to Calling, Reaching Out to Minority AIDS Victims."

Months after we'd begun utilizing my modified Shanti program in black neighborhoods, Simross had wanted to observe the group that was meeting with me. When I asked the attendees for their permission, they agreed but didn't want to be photographed or mentioned by name. They had reservations about disclosing their homosexuality in the daily newspaper. Lynn understood.

I've always taken the position that one announces one's sexual orientation whenever one chooses. That's a personal matter. I have no right to tell anyone when to make such a revelation. I determined that a public stance was necessary for me.

Lynn could see that my mission was all about reaching the minority community. When she asked if my community work was going to take the form of a secular agency, I answered yes and came up with a name—Minority AIDS Project or MAP, which was simple, easy to remember, and inclusive. Given the huge

Latino population in Central and South Central L.A., I knew that our organization had to serve all minority groups, not just blacks.

The article ended with this sentence: "Persons interested in assisting Bean with his AIDS outreach program, may call him at the following number . . ."

Not hundreds, but thousands of people flooded me with calls and letters. People were filled with fear, hungry for information, needy on every level imaginable. Some just needed to know that no, you can't contact AIDS through a cough or a sneeze or germs on a toilet seat. No, God doesn't hate homosexuals. No, AIDS is not God's punishment for being gay. Yes, intravenous drug users are at risk. Yes, women are at risk. Anyone can contract the virus through the exchange of bodily fluids.

Given the overwhelming community response, I didn't have a minute to waste. I had to establish MAP in a hurry. The Brotherhood Crusade, a community-based organization dedicated to addressing community needs, donated $1,500. I took the money, bought a couple of phones, and rented a small office. One of my church members, Christine Adams Tripp, began preparing an application for a 501(c)(3), a nonprofit tax-exempt organization. Lesley Burke, a registered nurse with a master's in public health and a master's in divinity, helped with those applications. Lesley has a razor-sharp memory of her involvement with MAP:

"I was working at Kaiser Hospital, supervising some seventy nurses, when I heard the doctors discussing GRID, the gay-related immune deficiency. Certain epidemiologists were eager to do research. That required volunteers, but the nurses were reluctant. Among themselves, they referred to homosexuals as 'queers' and 'fags' and wanted nothing to do with them. They were also afraid of being infected. Two things motivated me to volunteer—my oath as a nurse to care for the sick, and my Christian belief that it is a blessing and duty to serve the downtrodden. So when an unknown preacher named Carl Bean called the hospital to see if a nurse would come to a meeting of the Minority AIDS Project, I went to his little office in a broken-down building on Pico Boulevard.

"I saw his sincerity and signed up for the mission. In its initial stage, MAP was all about keeping people alive. AIDS patients, wearing paper gowns and paper shoes, were being discharged from hospitals. We'd pick them up and put them in hotel rooms until we could find shelters to house them. It was all about saving one life at a time. Many in the general community did not want to be identified with us for fear of being labeled gay. In the black community, homophobia was rampant. But we kept doing what we had to do. In those early years when we were this ragtag team running around the city doing anything to help AIDS patients with nowhere to turn, we were a band of guerrilla caretakers. Other than our core group of a half-dozen believers, we received little encouragement."

One early supporter was Maxine Waters, our state assemblywoman and a leading light of progressive politics. After reading the *L.A. Times* article, Ms. Walters called me. "Reverend Bean, you're the man we activists have been looking for," she said. "You're not afraid to address the catastrophic health issues that are threatening our community. I'm behind you all the way."

Ms. Waters made good on her word. When Jewel Williams, the wonderful woman who owned Catch One, the disco where I'd introduced "I Was Born This Way," sponsored a fund-raiser for MAP, Ms. Waters showed up and gave a rousing speech of support. "Reverend Bean is doing God's work," she said. "And that work is being carried out, day after day, night after night, in the hospitals of our community."

My hands-on hospital work galvanized not only my commitment to those who carried the virus but my fundamental relationship to Christ. I brought Him into those hospital rooms. Without him, I could never have done what I did. He was with me when I visited a patient at County Hospital. I was told that I had to put on a mask and refused, saying, "This man must see my face in order to see my faith. This man must see that I'm not afraid of him." Christ was with me when I opened the door and saw that there was practically nothing left of this dying man except his sunken eyes. His eyes said, "I am afraid. I am alone. I have been abandoned by the world."

The hospital workers had been so afraid to enter his room that his breakfast and lunch trays had been left in the hallway. Christ was with me when I entered the room, when I took the man into my arms, when his frail body collapsed into my chest. Christ was with me when I kissed his forehead, when I assured him that he was loved. Christ—the Christ of compassion, the Christ of forgiveness, the Christ of understanding—was with me when he whispered in my ear, "I am a father. I am a son. But my father and my son won't see me."

"Christ sees you," I said. "Christ is with you."

Christ was with me, Christ was holding me as I was holding him, healing our hearts, removing our fears, comforting our souls, the living Christ, the Christ of eternal hope. Christ was with me for every one of these stories. Christ was also with me when I met those patients who did not believe in him, who called themselves atheists and agnostics.

After the media started talking about me, I was invited by the organization Black and White Men Together to discuss the cultural similarities and differences of gay life in our various communities. There I met Chris Brownlee, a cultured and charming white man who was with his lover, Phil Wilson. After I had spoken about my church, Chris raised his hand and said, "Reverend, I doubt if I'd be welcomed."

"Why is that?"

"I was brought up in the Unitarian Universalist church. I'm essentially an agnostic."

"We'd love to have you worship the divine with us, Chris," I said.

"I don't worship the divine."

"You think, don't you?"

"All the time."

"Well, the miracle of thought is a divine gift. Besides, at our church we have no litmus tests. We don't care what you believe or don't believe. We welcome all. We love all. Our motto is, 'God is love and love is for everybody.' If you want to ignore that motto, that's fine with us. We're just pleased to have you there."

Next Sunday, Chris showed up at church. "Don't get any funny ideas, Carl," he said. "I'm not converting."

I laughed and said, "Be careful, though. There's the old story of the man who came to scoff and stayed to pray."

Eventually Chris lived that story. After many visits to Unity Fellowship, he told me, "Reverend, I haven't been able to shake that one statement you made about divine thought. Every time we think, that process connects us to the divine."

Chris began volunteering at our office. He hooked us up with our first computer and engineered our electronic office system. He also introduced me to Mike Weinstein, a young man who offered support when I took on the L.A. Board of Supervisors and demanded funding for those neglected HIV/AIDS patients in dire need. Mike began the AIDS Healthcare Foundation and the highly successful Out of the Closet thrift store chain that funded his foundation.

Tragically, Chris Brownlee had the virus. As it became full-blown AIDS, he was moved to a hospice. He asked that I come see him. He was clearly frightened. I held him in my arms.

"You are protected, Chris," I said. "You are surrounded by strong spirits. You are deeply loved."

He squeezed my hand and closed his eyes. A short time later, he rallied a bit and was released to the home that he and Phil shared in Silver Lake. He asked me to come by and visit. For the first time, he was eager to speak about God. He needed to tell me about his near-death experience.

"People are moving through my mind," he said.

"What do they look like?" I asked.

"They have no bodies," he said, "only faces."

"Faces," I repeated.

"Faces filled with light. Light begging me to come to them. When I reach them, though, they send me back. They say I'm not ready. But I'm not scared, Reverend. The light doesn't scare me."

"The light is beautiful," I said. "God is nothing but light. Nothing but love."

"Tell me more about God's love."

"The scripture says that perfect love casts out all fear."

"I believe it."

Chris died a few months later. Fittingly, the hospice where he had stayed was renamed in his honor. He was a brave warrior. He came to believe in a miraculous God who lifts fear from our hearts and, with mystic hands, gently wipes the perspiration from our brow.

It was 1987, and my finances—as well as MAP's—were bleak. I was six months behind in my home rent, ducking the landlord, coming in late and leaving early. They were about to shut off my gas and electricity. I was walking to the office because I couldn't afford a bus pass. My ministerial coat, bought secondhand, was so raggedy on the inside that I was ashamed to take it off, even when the heat of the day became too much. This was when God worked through everyday people I encountered.

At the supermarket, the checkout clerk saw me put back a can of tuna that I couldn't afford. When I got to the parking lot, the clerk, a white brother, ran after me. "Aren't you the preacher

I saw on TV talking about AIDS?" "Yes," I said. Then he whispered, "I'm sick. God bless you for what you're doing." And with that he slipped me a twenty-dollar bill, enabling me to take the bus to the office.

The next morning, I was on the bus again when an elderly black woman sat down next to me. "Here, son," she said, handing me a ten-dollar bill. "We're proud of you."

When I got to the office, I got a surprise message that a Mr. Robert Gordy was trying to reach me. Robert was Berry's brother and a high-ranking Motown executive.

"'I Was Born This Way' has taken off again," he said. "A dee-jay in New Jersey is playing it nonstop, and all the clubs in the tristate area are calling for you. This is the song that will not die. Are you willing to go back out there and perform?"

"Yes, sir," I said. "But I will only perform as Reverend Carl Bean, AIDS advocate. And I'll only perform in clerical garb."

"Great. Fly out this weekend."

"I want a thousand dollars each time I sing the song, Mr. Gordy. And if I'm called back to sing it again, I want another thousand."

"You'll get it."

Once again, God was right on time. With both me and MAP about to go under, "I Was Born This Way" came to our rescue. The epicenter of the song's revival was a club called the Zanzibar in Newark, New Jersey, that soulful community where I had once lived. The gay community in Newark had been devastated by AIDS, and "Born This Way" became a rallying cry for renewed hope. I proudly performed in a black suit and white clerical collar.

In Manhattan, I sang at Better Days, a gay disco. Each club seemed to be waiting for me. Professional dancers showed up and created an impromptu choreography around me. At discos in Connecticut and San Francisco, muscle-bound men in tank tops and shorts ran across the dance floor carrying colorful streamers. No matter how wild the scene, though, the message came through loud and clear.

Help me, Lord, tell the world that I was born this way!

The disco scene had changed. Musically, gospel and disco—along with tech—had all come together. For example, gospel singer Tramaine Hawkins had a number one club hit with "Fall Down," while the Clark Sisters, among the most popular gospel groups, had a smash called "You Brought the Sunshine (into My Life)" that was played in secular settings from coast to coast. I felt no separation between preaching in a club and in a church. I realized that my ministry had really begun the day that I stood in front of that microphone at Mo-West Studios in 1977 and declared to the world, "I Was Born This Way."

Only a month had passed from the day I had bought sardines because I couldn't afford tuna, and here I was, home from the disco tour with $20,000 in cash. MAP was back in business.

PADRE! PADRE!

Fear lives long and dies hard. Fear was what we faced on the front lines of AIDS. There were so many heartbreaking struggles with fear. One of my first clients at MAP was Darryl. He worked as Ray Charles's secretary and was also the organist at Reverend James Cleveland's Cornerstone Institutional Baptist Church. He was a great guy—brilliant, talented, witty, filled with life. The virus hit not only Darryl but many other members of the gospel-singing community, including Reverend Cleveland. These were loving lifetime friends of mine who were devout Christians.

Because same-sex-attracted men and women inside the church had been trained not to discuss their orientation in public, when AIDS became a public illness, many didn't know where to turn. Thus this terrible irony: churches built in the name of Jesus could not comfort their own members who were afflicted, downtrodden, and cast out by society. Their failure was due to the long-lingering hypocrisy that imposed on those members the terrible burden of hiding their sexuality.

The beautiful thing about the black church, though, was the love of Christ. I knew that love would prevail. In the world of Shanti, Jesus was not mentioned much, but in the neighborhoods where my sisters and brothers like Darryl were suffering, Jesus was everything.

"Jesus," I told Darryl, "died to rise again. Jesus is the ascended God-presence who cannot be kept down by anything."

Darryl died before his beloved preacher James Cleveland.

There are so many stories, so many miracles, so much overwhelming proof of the powerful peace God provides for all. First-time counselors, swearing they could never deal with such physical and emotional deterioration on the part of their "buddies," became stalwarts of steady support. Patients, furious with the way they had been left for dead, found gratitude when they received visits from people who had been trained to bring them loving attention.

The message spread. The Minority AIDS Project expanded, and the Latin American community came aboard. Transamerica gave us money to print our first brochure in both English and Spanish. Sensitive to many Latinos' Catholic heritage, I rewrote some of our material in order not to alienate them from God's all-encompassing love. Spanish-speaking gay men began contacting me, seeking information, guidance, and emotional support. I heard many stories of the horrific treatment—or lack of treatment—they were receiving at local clinics and hospitals. One hospital, afraid to deal with a patient, literally dumped him on the sidewalk outside our office on Pico. I had locked the door and closed down for the night when I saw a man outside in hospital pajamas and paper slippers. He was shivering and reaching out to me, crying, "Padre! Padre!" I took him in my arms, carried him up to our office, and called an ambulance to rush him to a hospital where a doctor familiar with our program guaranteed me that he would treat this man with the dignity he deserved.

On the political front, we were struggling but definitely surviving. I was blessed when Vera Owens joined the staff at MAP. She was my right hand and first secretary, a brave buddy and tireless worker who devoted countless hours to cooking meals, cleaning the homes, and providing spiritual solace to those suffering with the virus.

To get funding from the County Board of Supervisors, we made a strong case that MAP was the first and most skilled organization in L.A. County to deal with minority people carrying the virus. Much to our surprise, we faced vociferous opposition. A white woman from Orange County, together with an ultraconservative black woman, argued that their public service organization deserved the funding, not us. Claiming that we were pushing pornography, they showed the County Board of Supervisors pamphlets from an organization in San Francisco that they said was similar to MAP. These pamphlets showed explicit photographs bordering on the obscene. We made it clear that MAP would never tolerate such material; we considered it abhorrent and inappropriate. But the woman from Orange County claimed that because MAP was led by a gay man, it was producing exactly this kind of propaganda.

Thank God for Maxine Waters, then our state assemblywoman. Not only did she testify on my behalf in front of the board, but she brought along a group of distinguished black women—church and community leaders all—to testify as well. They came in their Sunday best—church hats and tailored suits—and, in no uncertain terms, told the supervisors that MAP was not only legitimate but absolutely necessary to the black community. We got the funding.

Meanwhile, Unity Fellowship of Christ Church got moving. We still had no building, but we had our commitment to God. The Cockatoo Inn, a motel and lounge on Imperial Highway in Hawthorne, south of Watts, that had always been friendly to gays, let us rent their meeting room for services. I conducted our first public service on Easter Sunday in front of some twenty or twenty-five worshippers, many of whom carried the virus.

"We are here to reconcile God's children to the love of Jesus

Christ," I preached. "God doesn't care if you're straight, gay, bi, or transgendered. God contains everything. God *is* everything. Here, on Easter morning, we have come to celebrate the Lord's victory over death. God's victory is our victory. God's resurrection is our resurrection. God's eternal love is our eternal love. We are crucified as God is crucified. We rise as God rises. God is in us. We are in God. God lives. We live. Now and forever. Glory to the living God! Glory to the risen Christ!"

The Cockatoo Inn proved too far away for many of my congregants, so we found another home in the Ebony Showcase Theatre on Washington Boulevard, in L.A.'s midcity black neighborhood. Back in the day, the Ebony had presented superstars from Sammy Davis Jr. to Eartha Kitt, but by the eighties, it had fallen on hard times, and its owners, Mr. and Mrs. Nick Stewart, were struggling to keep it afloat. They graciously allowed us to hold services there. There was something satisfying and familiar about preaching in a theater. In fact, I had dreamed of preaching in a theater! The setting also brought to mind Vinnette and the Urban Arts Corps. She had been an advocate of theater from the heart. "Theater," she used to say, "is an arena in which we search for the truth. There is nothing phony about theater. Executed on the highest level, theater is a spiritual experience." The Ebony was definitely spiritual.

"Please close your eyes," I told the congregation, "and hear these words. You are unique. No one else has your eyes, or your mouth; no one else has your smile, or your way of walking or talking. God made you one of a kind. Gay, straight, bi, transgendered—you are God's precious creation. God loves you unconditionally. God loves you endlessly. Think about that. Feel that. Breathe in God's love.

"Now slowly open your eyes and walk around this church and tell everyone you see, 'You are very special.' Give your neighbor a hug and speak the words from your heart. Look him or her in the eyes and say, 'You are very special.'"

Everyone got up, joyfully recited this affirmation, and hugged one another. Everyone said it over and over again until the theater rang with the words, "You are very special. You are very special. Yes, you are very special." That affirmation became a central and permanent part of our worship.

From my days as a child, studying under Reverend Wood at Providence Baptist in Baltimore, I knew that the Bible was the backbone of any black Christian service. Thus I made certain that Unity Fellowship approached scripture with a heart that sought the all-encompassing nature of God's miraculous grace. Scripture was there to heal our pain, not create fear. And of course there was music—always music. We bonded together in songs, just as our ancestors had sung before us. Our choir was small in number but powerful in spirit. The worshippers, grateful for a church that accepted their sexual orientation, responded. One brother with the virus was so thrilled by the experience that he bought fifty Bibles and donated them to the church.

Ebony, though, had its problems. When the leaky roof and the stench of booze from the Saturday night parties held in the same space became too much for us, we moved on. Jewel Williams was our rock. After every service, she invited the full congregation, many of whom were suffering with AIDS, to her club, Catch One, where the cook, James, prepared a bountiful meal for everyone. If someone was homeless, I had only to call Jewel, who secured a clean room for that woman or man. If our church had no place to worship, Jewel opened the doors of Catch One, which became our sanctuary. In fact, it was Jewel's sister, a real estate agent, who found us a permanent location. The building at Jefferson and Sycamore had housed a health clinic, and the doctor who ran it was only too eager to turn it over to our church and to MAP. He was gratified that we would be serving the community's critical medical needs.

In our new home, our services expanded. At the end of the

work week, I conducted a Friday night testimony service. It was a beautiful and healing ritual. I even loved the preparation—setting up the chairs, turning off the lights, lighting the candles. As the men and women entered, many of whom were living with the virus, they saw the flickering candles and heard the sound of tropical rain or ocean waves. I played ambient sound tapes that gently calmed the soul. For a long time, we sat in silence. The Self-Realization Fellowship had taught me the value of quietude. After a half hour of meditation, I invited worshippers to tell their stories. The stories were amazing, heartbreaking, and inspiring. There were young people and old people, people from the Bahamas and Cuba who, because of their homosexuality, had been disowned by their families and churches. There were people without green cards, without homes, without direction, and without hope. Now, in a church led by Christ, they were given their voice. They could speak as long as they needed to. They could feel accepted and appreciated. With no need to apologize or hide, they could be their true selves.

In time, I was blessed to have students in the field of liberation theology, some of whom became colleagues. Zachary Jones became my first assistant pastor and eventually set up the first Unity Fellowship satellite church in New York City. Word spread. Every week we had visitors from around the country and the world. Even Dr. C. Everett Koop, the surgeon general under President Reagan, was eager to learn about our work in L.A. He brought me to Philadelphia to help prepare the national mailer on AIDS that went to every home in America. Along with entertainers like Dionne Warwick and Natalie Cole, Koop became a major MAP supporter.

Our churches multiplied. We opened Unity Fellowship congregations in Brooklyn and Detroit. In the past quarter century, our ministry has expanded exponentially. Today we have four jurisdictions—the West, for our churches in L.A., Long

Beach, Riverside, and San Diego; the East, for Buffalo, Detroit, Brooklyn, and Rochester; the Mid-Atlantic, for Baltimore, New Brunswick, Newark, and Philadelphia; and the South for Atlanta, Charlotte, and Washington, D.C.

As the church expanded, I was being pulled in many directions. I was being called to AIDS conferences around the country, even as my pastoring responsibilities—officiating at funerals, keeping up with hospital visits—grew. I needed help. Thus we established a House of Bishops. I was elected the first prelate, and Zachary Jones became our second bishop. Today we have two female bishops—Jacquelyn Holland in Newark and Tanya Rawls in Charlotte—and a national staff that oversees our policies. The culmination of our growth came some years ago at a service at the National Cathedral in Washington, D.C., where I was consecrated archbishop. What a blessing! My family came up from Baltimore. My friends came from around the country. AIDS organizations from several different countries were represented. Our mass choir, by then 250 strong, brought down the heavens. High-ranking officials from the NAACP and the Urban League were in attendance. Dr. Randall Bailey, the Andrew W. Mellon professor of Hebrew Bible at the Interdenominational Theological Center in Atlanta, officiated and preached the consecration sermon. The service itself had all the diverse dynamics of our culture—African dance, glorious gospel music, fabulous preaching, and a church of worshippers filled with gratitude.

FROM BLOOD TO BLOOD

The people I've met on my walk with Christ have heartwarming stories. I've always spoken my truth so that those I've encountered might speak theirs. I've expressed my conviction that, though fear is part of life, fear need not rule our minds or restrict our hearts. I've advocated for love beyond the narrow restrictions of specific language or theology. I've spoken about my emergence from a closet of secrecy and pain in the hope of inspiring others. I've reached people who are gay, straight, transgendered, bi, black, white, yellow, and brown. They come from backgrounds of both privilege and poverty. A disciple of whom I'm particularly proud is Victor McKamy, a straight man and former member of the Bloods, an infamous gang. Today, with a summa cum laude master's degree in public education, he has succeeded me as executive director of the Minority Aids Project. He recently told a group of MAP supporters how, in a most improbable way, my story dramatically shaped his.

"I'm a product of South Central," he began. "In 1979, at age twelve, I joined the Bloods as a second-generation member. The first-generation Bloods used knives; our generation picked up the guns and raised the level of violence. We didn't care who we hurt or how we hurt them. We were family, representing our neighborhood, protecting our turf. The other dudes used gang names. I was bold enough to use my real name—Vic. I didn't care who knew. Small in stature, I fought for my respect. The more ferocious my behavior, the more respect I got. By tenth grade I was in the criminal justice system for having stabbed a classmate. Not long after that, I was caught with a loaded sawed-off shotgun on my way to murder a rival. I was imprisoned for nearly four years in a facility where Crips outnumbered us Bloods six to one. The Crips put rat poison and ejaculated in our food, but somehow I survived. I muscled my way through. When Mom visited me and said, 'I wish I could do this time for you,' her words got to me. I knew I had to clear my head and change my heart.

"By then I was nineteen. My closest friend, a brother Blood, had been murdered on the streets. I grabbed a gun and was on my way to retaliate when the cops stopped me. The judge sent me away again, but this time to a facility with an education program. I studied history and theology and discovered that Jesus was hardly a punk. He was a radical who took on authority. I related.

"When I got out, I was put into a reentry program where I heard about how AIDS was attacking our community. I still wanted to represent my neighborhood, but this time I wanted to do it righteously. Reverend Carl Bean was introduced to us as someone who loved the community enough to try and save it. When he spoke to us, he did so with absolute candor. There was nothing phony about him. He went right to the point: 'We need you. Your people need you.' When I joined up as a MAP worker, I got flak from some friends who called me a fag for hanging out with fags. I quickly learned not to care what anyone said. I knew Reverend Bean was up to good. He had brains and he had guts. He walked with me into the most dangerous projects in South Central, where we gave red condoms to Bloods and blue ones to Crips. We went door to door in run-down complexes where murderers were known to live. It didn't matter to Reverend. The man had a job to do, and he did it.

"In the midnineties, the demand for AIDS care increased exponentially. Our services were desperately needed by thousands of people suffering with the virus, but our resources were depleted. We were virtually broke, and our sources for funding had gone dry. Reverend's reaction was to declare a public fast for himself. He didn't eat for weeks. His fast attracted the media, and the story brought us the donations we needed to keep going.

"Aside from benefiting from Reverend's professional leadership, I could also talk to him about my personal problems. We got so close I began calling him 'Dad.' As a macho guy, I never believed in a million years that I would have an intimate emotional relationship with a gay man. With Reverend, though, it was never about sex; it was about your humanity and how to expand your generosity of spirit. I was so inspired by his example of service, I said, 'Dad, one day I'm going to take over your office.' 'Great,' he said. 'First get your education, then you'll get this office.'

"I worked at MAP, learning every aspect of its operation. At the same time, I went to school. After ten years of study, I showed Dad my master's degree. That very day he packed up and turned his office over to me. He made good on his word. He always does. I was raised in this organization, just as I was raised in Dad's Unity Fellowship of Christ Church. I've seen miracles in many forms. I was cleansed by the blood of Christ. I've brought my Blood brothers to meet Dad and, after he spoke, watched them break down in tears. I've seen him father—and mother—people who were adamant about their atheism, their determination to refuse help, or their hatred of homosexuality. Another time when MAP didn't have enough money to keep the doors open, I saw Dad sell the physical building that housed his church. 'We'll find somewhere else to meet,' he said. 'Meanwhile, we got to keep reaching those patients.' That's Reverend Bean, who, with his story, inspired me to rewrite mine."

———

I have at times found my role as a pastoral counselor brutally trying. One day in my MAP office, for instance, a young, beautiful African American woman, who had attended church her entire life and graduated from college, sat before me and said, "But I saved myself for him. I did exactly what the Bible said. I followed the teachings of my preacher, my mom and dad. I was proud that the white I wore on my wedding day was authentic. I was a virgin. So why me? Why did my husband infect me with this virus? Why is God punishing me?"

I knew a glib answer wouldn't work. I knew I had to let her get it all out. I remained silent and let her speak. I remembered the importance of listening with my heart, not my head. She told me that her brother, a law enforcement officer, wanted to kill her husband, and it was only their dad who restrained him.

"I'll never be with a man again," she said. "I'm mad at the church, at God, at everyone. Help me, Rev. Help me."

I began talking to her about a God who creates us all with free will. I said, "Sweetheart, we are not puppets. Because of love, we were created with the ability to reason. We've all used our free will in wrong ways and made bad choices. But don't blame yourself. None of us can know completely what is going on with our loved ones. We don't know all their shortcomings. We can't see all their frailties. Your husband may not have known that he was infected. That's why we are here. It is important that all sexually active people today know their status. That's the only way we can prevent things like this from continuing to happen in our community. No one is to blame for this virus. No one deserves to be infected. I'd like to assign you a personal buddy, someone who will be a confidante and friend. You can call her night or day; you can have lunch with her, go to the movies, or just sit and talk. You can be assured that this is a person who understands. Is that okay with you?"

"I can't tell you how much that means to me, Rev."

"God bless you, Daughter. And remember, I'm only a phone call away, but God is even closer."

Another client came in to ask me how to tell his partner that he was positive. This was an especially painful story because, in his reluctance to reveal his status, the man had continued not to use a condom with his partner.

"Son," I said, "it is imperative that we make your lover aware of what may be happening to his body. If you can't do this alone, bring him to my pastoral office and I'll assist you."

"Please, Rev, I've been going out of my mind."

"If you give me permission, I'll dial his number and invite him to my office immediately."

I did. The partner came to MAP, and I helped them deal with the truth.

Because of my ministerial role, a deeply religious middle-aged Hispanic husband and wife were referred to me through their County Hospital social worker. They spoke little English. He had full-blown AIDS and she was also infected. I went to their small apartment in East L.A. Even with my limited Spanish, it was clear that the most important thing to him was to make her believe his infection was the result of a mosquito bite. I knew my job was to assure them that in their current situation God had not abandoned them. As I looked around the apartment and saw their icons and candles, I talked about Jesus' profound love for all his children. I spoke of Mother Mary and Our Lady of Guadalupe. I accompanied them to the MAP office, where Spanish-speaking workers registered them as clients and explained the full range of our services. In the process, I learned that, to survive economically, the husband had sold himself to affluent men in show business who cruised Santa Monica Boulevard for anonymous sex. I never told the wife his true source of infection and made sure that MAP helped them in every way, including in their final days.

Some weeks I officiated at three or four funerals a day. I conducted services at every single funeral home in South Central L.A. My spirituality was stretched as never before. At the end of a day, I'd go back to the MAP office on Jefferson and work on administrative details until three or four in the morning. Because I didn't have a car, I'd call a taxi to take me home, but the cab companies all refused to travel deep into the black section of the city at that hour. One driver, though, always came through. He was an Indian gentleman from New Delhi who sensed the urgency of my work. When I left the office, he'd beam his headlights on MAP's front door to make sure I locked up safely. When he got to my home, he waited until I was inside before driving off. Never failing to answer my calls, he was part of the reason I was able to persevere. I was certain God had sent him.

My hospital visits were intense. Invariably, people would see me in the hallways and call me over. "Reverend, I know who you are. My son is dying of AIDS. Please come speak to him. Please come pray with us." I could not turn down such a request. Sometimes those sessions would last for hours, but I could not walk out on a suffering patient.

I was once at a hospital when a Jewish woman approached me and said, "My husband is dying. He needs you." "Is it AIDS?" I asked. "No, cancer." "Almost all my work has been devoted to AIDS patients," I said. "That doesn't matter," she answered. "He needs some kind of spiritual connection. I can feel in your spirit that you can comfort people. Please comfort my husband." I went in and sat with the man, listening to his fears, holding his hand, assuring him that death was a beginning, not an end.

Another white sister came up to me in the halls of UCLA Hospital and said, "Father, will you give my husband his last rites?" "I'm not a priest, I'm not Catholic, " I said. "That doesn't matter, Father. He needs to confess." I went in the room, put on a communion cloth, and told the elderly man that I was there to listen and to love him. He confessed his deceitful business practices; then he confessed his sexual infidelities. When he was through, I could see his anxious eyes grow peaceful and calm.

A family who lived in Little Tokyo contacted me about a Buddhist funeral service they were having for their son who died of AIDS. I said that I didn't know the required ritual prayers. They said that it didn't matter. They had seen me speak at the Greek Theater, where the city of Los Angeles had held ecumenical public meetings on the AIDS crisis. "We know you belong at our service," the family said. "We know that you will bring the spirit with you."

These encounters showed me the transcendence of the divine. While suffering, these people asked for my hand. I took theirs and, once again, was taught about the universality of compassion, understanding, and unconditional love.

GRACE AND MERCY

Prestigious organizations have recognized our work. It was a blessing to receive the NAACP Image Award, the SCLC Prophetic Witness Award, and the Social Justice Ministry Award from the National Council of Negro Women. We've been given plaques and ribbons, trophies and public acknowledgment on national TV, all of which bring attention to our cause, underscoring our conviction that God is love and love is for everybody.

Both MAP and Unity Fellowship survived. The gay community survived. But even though education became more widespread and the drugs grew more effective, HIV/AIDS remains a hugely destructive force. It is still robbing men, women, and children of their very lives. The need for treatment is greater than ever. So is the need for love.

As I look back over this journey, starting with my innocent days as a little boy running the streets of Baltimore, I see how love sustained me—love from my biological mother, my grandmothers, my godparents, my friends, my preachers, my doctor in University Hospital, love from gospel singers and stage directors, love from record producers and disco owners, love born out of a need for a connection, a need to feel worthy and wanted.

I preach every Sunday. I preach out of the Bible, out of my life and the lives of my parishioners. I tell my congregation, "Look, I'm an old queen who knows something about promiscuity. I've been to the bathhouses, I've been to the parks, I've been to every cruise scene imaginable. I've done it all, and I've done it twice. And if I've survived, it's because God wants to tell you that promiscuity ain't gonna fill that hole in your soul. The bathhouse will not wash you clean. Crazy sex just makes you crazier. The fun don't last and the health risks get riskier. That party's over. But another party has begun. That party goes on forever. That party isn't about getting high on happy pills or some naked body; that party is about finding joy—real joy, sustaining joy, eternal joy. We're all invited to that party—every last one of us. That's the party we're having this morning, the party celebrating God, praising God, lifting God, giving God our burdens and, in turn, accepting God's grace."

I continue to pray for the safety of gay, lesbian, transgendered people—and anyone made to feel "less than." As someone who grew up an effeminate child in urban America, I know the horror of turning the wrong corner and suddenly being attacked. I'll never forget how, at age fourteen, an older boy assaulted me for being gay. As a result, I wound up with a broken arm. I couldn't tell my godparents the truth and had to make up an excuse. Untold numbers of my brothers and sisters have been beaten, raped, and murdered because they could not or would not hide their sexual identities. There are millions of innocent people, young and old, who must live with this constant fear. My prayer is that the family of man can learn to accept the diversity in God's creation.

As a servant of God within the HIV/AIDS community for the past thirty years, I look back at the people I was blessed to encounter. Some survived. Many didn't. How many times was my heart completely shattered when an old gospel singer from back in the day approached me? He or she was gay. He or she had attended a black church. But he or she, once struck by the virus, had been shunned. Many churches would not shelter or support the very musical souls who had brought to their worship services much of its mystical spirit.

"Reverend," I'd hear over and over again, "does God hate me because I'm gay?"

"No, my son," I'd say. "You can only be who God created you to be."

"Reverend," the cry would continue, "does God hate me because I'm a lesbian . . . or transgendered . . . or bisexual . . . or black . . . or poor . . . or sick with disease?"

"No, my children. It is not God who causes us to live as outcasts. In their quest for power and position, human beings create categories to elevate themselves and belittle others. If we accept the world's scorn, we grow weak. If we accept God's love, we grow strong. I promise this, I know this. My life is testimony to one statement and one statement only—God is love, and love is for everyone."

ACKNOWLEDGMENTS

Archbishop Bean thanks:

Mom and Dad, Harry and Jeter, for loving me, providing for me, and teaching me the meaning of family

My sister Martha, my best friend

My great nieces Cori and Kia, whom I love with all my heart

Tony, Carla, and Darryl

Cousins Carroll and Andrew

My grandmother Mary, Aunt Rosalie, and all my relatives

Lillie Jackson, my mentor

Reverend Marcus Garvey Wood and his wife Aunt Bessy

Mr. and Mrs. Leslie Wood

Mrs. Marian Smith, choir/music teacher extraordinaire

Reverend Dr. Samuel De Witt Proctor

My musical father, the great Alex Bradford

My artistic mother, Vinnette Justine Carroll

All the kids who embraced me and made me feel a loving part of our world—the east side gang on Layfayette and Chapel and the west side gang on Lauretta and Bentalou

My classmates throughout the Baltimore school systems, earliest singing buddies, whether doo-wopping on the corner or singing gospel in church

My fellow drum majors and majorettes

My childhood gay, lesbian, bi and transgendered friends

Bishop William Morris O'Neill

Estelle Brown and family

Jackie Verdell, Ruth Davis, and the Davis Sisters

Calvin White and the Gospel Wonders

Joe Bostic Jr. and Joe Bostic Sr.

The Apollo Theater, the Rockland Palace, and all the Harlem performance venues

The Brill Building and 1650 Broadway composers and producers

The New York theater community

Ellis Haslip

ACKNOWLEDGMENTS

Lawrence Lucie
Hope Clarke
Micki Grant
Mary Alice
The gay, lesbian, bi and transgendered New Yorkers who touched my life
Imogene Green, the Gospel Chimes, and the entire Chicago gospel community
Greater Abyssinian Baptist family
My other Newark family, Dee Dee and Dionne Warwick, mother Lee and father Mancel
Cissy Houston and the Drinkard clan
Judy Clay
Lee Young Sr., my L.A. dad
Lee Young Jr.
The Chairman, Berry Gordy, his sister Gwen, his niece Iris, his brother Robert, and the Motown family
ABC records
Bunny Jones and Chris Spierer, for writing "I Was Born This Way"
Reverend James Cleveland, the King of Gospel
Reverend Troy Perry, my constant friend
Reverend Chip Murray, a lion in our community
Reverend Joseph Lowry and Mrs. Lowry
Henry Jackson, my best L.A. friend
Mrs. Coretta Scott King
SCLC
NAACP
Kevin
Sherwood
Universal Love
Albert Gordon, whose legal expertise and compassionate heart helped our cause immeasurably
Harry Hay
Morris Kight
James Baldwin
Bayard Rustin
Audre Lorde
Ruth Ellis
Jewel Williams
Mr. and Mrs. Nick Stewart
Vera Owens
Christian Tripp

Bob Smith
Phil Wilson
Chris Brownley
Paul Kawata
Ivy Bottini
Elizabeth Taylor
Elton John
The National Minority AIDS Council
The great Dorothy Irene Height of the National Council of Negro Women
Dr. C. Everett Koop
All the early pioneers in the fight against AIDS
Congresswoman Maxine Waters
Congresswoman Dianne Watson
Supervisor Yvonne Burke
Supervisor Kenneth Hahn
Supervisor Mark Ridley Thomas
Councilman Herb Wesson Jr.
Councilwoman Wendy Greuel
Mayor Tom Bradley
Mayor Antonio Villaraigosa
My dear friend, Jackie Goldberg
Danny Bakewell and the Brotherhood Crusade
Los Angeles Sentinel
Brenda Marsh
Dr. Wilbert Jordan
Tony Heilbut
David Nathan
KJLH
All the mothers, fathers, sisters, and brothers who fought with me to establish the Minority AIDS Project and everyone who has helped MAP raise funds
Every bishop, pastor, clergy person, deacon, choir member and parishioner of the Los Angeles mother church and the entire Unity Fellowship Church movement
Simon & Schuster, who made this book possible
To the folk who call me "Dad," I love you with all my heart
David Ritz, his wife Roberta, and his family
To D.C., the love of my life who shares my every moment
And to all of you who have crossed over, yes, all the ancestors

ACKNOWLEDGMENTS

David Ritz thanks:

    Archbishop Carl Bean

    Dejon Mayes, my dear who introduced me to Carl and made this book possible

    Robert Ritz, for superb creative assistance

    David Rosenthal

    David Vigliano

    Ruth Fecych

    Michelle Rourke

    Daughters Alison and Jessica, sons Henry and Jim, granddaughter Charlotte, grandsons Alden and James

    Father Milton

    Sisters Esther and Elizabeth

    All my beautiful nephews, nieces, and cousins

    Pals Alan Eisenstock and Harry Weinger

Printed in the United States
By Bookmasters